BREAKING THE CHAINS OF THE PAST

BREAKING THE CHAINS OF THE PAST

A COMPLETE GUIDE TO RECOVERING AND HEALING FROM INHERITED FAMILY TRAUMA AND EMOTIONALLY IMMATURE PARENTS (2-IN-1 COLLECTION)

GENERATIONAL HEALING

BOOK 3

ESSIE WOODARD

May this book serve as a key to unlock the secrets of your past and a compass to guide you toward a future of understanding, resilience, and emotional freedom. Here's to breaking the chains of the past and forging a path of light for generations to come.

Healing comes from taking responsibility: to realize that it is you - and no one else - that creates your thoughts, your feelings, and your actions.

— PETER SHEPHERD

CONTENTS

ANCESTRAL SHADOWS

HOW TO DEAL WITH EMOTIONALLY IMMATURE PARENTS

ANCESTRAL SHADOWS

UNRAVELING THE HIDDEN IMPACT OF INHERITED FAMILY TRAUMA AND THE PATH TO RECOVERY

THE ECHOES OF OUR ANCESTORS

Unveiling the Legacy of the Past

In the stillness of our private moments, we often find ourselves grappling with emotions and fears that seem to have been with us longer than our memories can account for. Within the intricate tapestry of our family history, we may find the threads of these unaccounted feelings—strands of inherited family trauma that have been woven into our being across generations.

The concept of inherited family trauma is not merely a metaphor for the shared experiences within a family lineage. It is a phenomenon that has garnered attention from psychologists, geneticists, and sociologists alike. It suggests that the traumas of our forebears—the wars they waged, the losses they suffered, the adversities they overcame—do not perish with them. Instead, these experiences can leave an indelible mark on the psyche and even the genetic makeup of subsequent generations.

As we embark on this journey of understanding, it is essential to acknowledge the complexity of trauma. Trauma is not a singular event but a cascade of responses that ripple through one's life, often surfacing unexpectedly. It can manifest as a heightened state of anxiety, a predisposition to depression, or an inexplicable sense of grief. We look to the past for their origins when these symptoms arise without a direct cause.

The legacy of the past is only sometimes visible. Like the roots of a tree, it stretches deep and wide, hidden beneath the surface. Only through the careful excavation of family stories, patterns, and behaviors can we begin to unearth the impact of what has been passed down to us. This legacy can be a source of strength, imbuing us with resilience and wisdom. Yet, it can also be a burden, a silent weight we carry, often without realizing its source.

In the following pages, we will delve into the heart of what defines inherited family trauma. We will explore the mechanisms through which trauma is transmitted, the signs that suggest its presence, and how we can confront and heal from these inherited wounds. The journey requires courage and vulnerability, which involves confronting the shadows of our family's past. Yet, through this confrontation, we can emerge with a deeper understanding of ourselves and a renewed capacity for healing and growth.

As we stand on the precipice of this exploration, let us do so with empathy for those who came before us and with a commitment to breaking the cycles that may have held us back. The echoes of our ancestors carry with them stories of pain and perseverance, and it is our task to listen, learn, and liberate ourselves from the silent repercussions of their experiences.

Defining Inherited Family Trauma

At its core, inherited family trauma refers to the transference of emotional and psychological consequences from one generation to the next. This transmission is not merely about the retelling of stories or the conscious emulation of behaviors; it is an enigmatic process by which the unresolved traumas of our forebears—be they wrought by war, displacement, loss, or abuse—echo within us, influencing our behaviors, our relationships, and even our health.

The concept of inherited trauma suggests that the experiences of our ancestors can leave an imprint on the genetic material they pass down to us. This concept challenges the traditional boundaries of what we consider heritable. It is not just the color of our eyes or the shape of our nose that we inherit from our parents and their parents before them; we may also inherit a propensity for anxiety, an inclination toward specific fears, or a susceptibility to depression.

This inheritance is not one of conscious choice. Children do not select which traits or burdens they receive, nor do parents intentionally bestow their unresolved pains upon their offspring. Yet, the emotional legacies of those who came before us can be as much a part of our inheritance as the physical attributes we see in the mirror.

Inherited family trauma is not a deterministic sentence, however. Recognizing its presence is the first step toward healing and transformation. By bringing these inherited patterns into the light of awareness, we can understand their influence and, with compassion and courage, work to resolve the pain unwittingly passed down through the generations.

As we delve deeper into this exploration, we will uncover the intricate ways these traumas are transmitted and the profound implications they hold for our understanding of self, relationships with others, and collective well-being. With each step on this journey, we strive to honor the experiences of those who came before us, not as a burden but as a call to healing and growth for ourselves and future generations.

The Science of Transmission

The concept of inherited family trauma hinges on the understanding that the emotional and psychological scars of one generation can be passed down to the next, not merely through the stories shared at the dinner table, but through a more silent and pervasive medium: our very biology.

The science of transmission, in the context of inherited family trauma, is a relatively new frontier that straddles the realms of genetics, psychology, and neurobiology. It is a field that seeks to unravel the complex mechanisms by which the effects of trauma are transmitted across generations. To comprehend this phenomenon, we must delve into the realm of epigenetics, a branch of science that studies how the expression of genes can be altered without changing the genetic code itself.

Epigenetics has illuminated that environmental factors, including trauma, can lead to chemical modifications around the genes. These modifications can affect how genes are turned on or off, and remarkably, some of these epigenetic changes can be passed down to offspring. This means that the child of a person who has experienced profound trauma might inherit a predisposition for specific stress responses, even if the child does not directly experience the trauma itself.

Moreover, the transmission of trauma can also occur through learned behaviors and patterns within the family. Children often learn how to respond to the world around them by observing their parents. If a parent has developed certain behaviors as a result of trauma—such as hypervigilance, anxiety, or avoidance—these behaviors can become the blueprint for the child's responses to stress and adversity.

The interplay between these inherited epigenetic changes and learned behaviors creates a complex web of influences that can shape an individual's emotional landscape. It is a silent legacy that can manifest subtly yet profoundly, from heightened stress responses to how one navigates relationships and copes with challenges.

Understanding the science of transmission is not just an academic exercise; it carries profound implications for therapy and healing. By recognizing that the echoes of our ancestors' experiences may reverberate within us, we can begin to unravel these threads and seek to heal not only ourselves but potentially prevent the perpetuation of trauma in future generations.

As we continue to explore the depths of inherited family trauma, it is essential to consider the historical contexts that have shaped the collective experiences of entire populations. The traumas of war, displacement, and oppression do not fade with time; instead, they can leave an indelible mark on the descendants of those who directly endured such hardships. Within this broader historical framework, we can further understand the individual narratives of inherited trauma and the resilience that often emerges in the face of such enduring legacies.

Historical Contexts of Inherited Trauma

As we delve into the historical contexts of inherited trauma, we begin to understand that the experiences of our ancestors are not merely relics of the past but are intricately linked to our present lives. The notion that the emotional and psychological scars of one generation can imprint themselves onto the next is a concept that has gained increasing recognition and understanding.

To comprehend the full impact of inherited trauma, we must first acknowledge the myriad events that have left indelible marks on entire populations. Wars, genocides, slavery, and natural disasters are but a few cataclysmic occurrences that have shaped the collective psyche of affected groups. The suffering endured by those who lived through such harrowing times does not simply vanish with their passing. Instead, the effects can ripple through generations, manifesting in many ways, from psychological predispositions to behavioral patterns.

Consider, for example, the descendants of those who survived the

Holocaust. Research has shown that the children and even grandchildren of survivors often carry with them an unconscious legacy of fear, anxiety, and vigilance despite never having encountered such threats themselves. Similarly, the offspring of those who have been subjected to the brutality of slavery may inherit a deep-seated wariness and mistrust, a survival mechanism once necessary for their ancestors' very existence.

The historical contexts of inherited trauma are not limited to these large-scale atrocities. Personal and familial traumas, such as domestic violence, abuse, or the sudden loss of a loved one, can also imprint upon the family narrative. These private agonies, though perhaps not as widely acknowledged, can be just as potent in their ability to shape the lives of future generations.

It is essential to recognize that the transmission of trauma is not a simple cause-and-effect process. It is a complex interplay of genetic, environmental, social, and cultural factors. How trauma is expressed and processed—or not processed—within a family or community can significantly influence how it is carried forward. The silence around suffering, for instance, can create an environment where the pain is internalized, and its expression is stifled, leaving subsequent generations to grapple with unspoken legacies.

As we consider the historical contexts of inherited trauma, we also begin to see the resilience that is passed down alongside the pain. Stories of survival, overcoming, and strength in the face of adversity are also part of the legacy handed down. These narratives of resilience are crucial, for they offer hope and a pathway toward healing. They remind us that while the past cannot be changed, the future is unwritten, and there is power in acknowledging and addressing the echoes of our ancestors.

In this light, understanding the historical contexts of inherited trauma is not merely an academic exercise; it is a vital step in the journey toward healing. By recognizing the origins of our inherited pain, we can start to unravel the complex web of influences that shape our lives and begin the process of reclaiming our stories. This knowledge paves the way for us to approach the next steps with a sense of purpose and possibility as we seek to transform the legacy of trauma into one of understanding, growth, and renewal.

Setting the Stage for Healing

Now, as we stand at the threshold of understanding, it is time to illuminate the path toward healing. The recognition of inherited family trauma is not an end but a beginning—a point of departure from which we can embark on a transformative journey. This journey is about tracing the scars of the past and learning how to heal them in the present and prevent their perpetuation into the future.

Healing inherited trauma requires a multifaceted approach. It begins with acknowledging the pain passed down, often obscured by the mists of time. To set the stage for healing, we must first create a space of safety and acceptance where these inherited wounds can be gently revealed and explored. This space is not just physical but emotional and psychological—a sanctuary within ourselves and our communities where vulnerability is not a liability but a bridge to deeper understanding.

Empathy is the cornerstone of this healing process. It allows us to connect with our ancestors' experiences, feel the weight of their burdens, and offer them the compassion they may never have received. Through empathy, we can begin to disentangle our own identity from the legacy of trauma, recognizing that while it has shaped us, it does not define us.

Analytical reflection is equally important. It involves a careful examination of the patterns that trauma has woven into our family narratives. We can identify how these patterns have influenced our beliefs, behaviors, and relationships by understanding them. This understanding empowers us to make conscious choices about which threads we wish to carry forward and which we choose to release.

The journey of healing is not linear. It ebbs and flows, with moments of profound insight and periods of quiet growth. It requires patience, for the work of untangling generations of trauma cannot be rushed. It demands courage, for confronting the pain of the past can be daunting. And it necessitates hope—a belief in the possibility of change and the potential for renewal.

As we embark on this journey, we are not alone. We walk alongside those who have come before us, guided by their stories and strengthened by their spirit. And we walk with each other, sharing the common bond of humanity that transcends time and place.

In setting the stage for healing, we are not merely addressing the echoes of our ancestors. We are shaping the legacy we will leave for those who follow. It is a profound responsibility and a precious opportunity to weave a new pattern in the tapestry of our lineage—one that honors the past while forging a future defined by healing, resilience, and love.

1

THE WEBS WE WEAVE: PATTERNS OF TRAUMA

Identifying Patterns in Family Histories

The exploration of family histories is akin to the work of an archeologist, sifting through layers of time to uncover the artifacts of past traumas. These traumas, whether they be events of war, displacement, abuse, or loss, do not dissipate with the passing of those who first endured them. Instead, they can imprint themselves upon the psyche of subsequent generations, manifesting in behaviors, beliefs, and emotional responses that seem disconnected from the immediate experiences of those who carry them.

To identify these patterns, we must first acknowledge the resilience and the suffering of those who came before us. It is a delicate balance to honor their strength while recognizing the wounds they could not heal. In doing so, we begin to see how specific themes recur: a grandparent's unspoken grief mirrored in a parent's inability to express love, or a great-aunt's experience of abandonment echoed in the pervasive loneliness of her descendants.

These patterns are not always negative; they can also be sources of strength and survival. A family's legacy of overcoming adversity may inspire courage and determination in the face of modern challenges. However, when the inherited patterns are maladaptive, they can lead to a cycle of pain that perpetuates until acknowledged and addressed.

We must approach our family histories with empathy and a critical eye in identifying these patterns. We must listen to the stories with an understanding that memory is often selective and subjective. We must recognize the filters through which these stories are told and retold, shaped by cultural norms, personal biases, and the human tendency to create coherence out of chaos.

Through this process, we begin to map out the emotional landscape of our lineage. We may discover that a tendency towards anxiety is not simply a personal challenge but a thread that has run through our family for generations. Or we may find that our difficulty with trust and intimacy is not an isolated struggle but part of a broader familial pattern of insecure attachments.

As we chart these patterns, we prepare the ground for the work of healing. We can start to untangle the webs woven through our families by bringing these inherited traumas into the light. We can begin to differentiate which parts of our emotional inheritance are ours to carry and which we can lay down, breaking the cycle for ourselves and future generations.

This work is not done in isolation. In the context of our relationships—those intimate attachments that shape our lives—we often find the most apparent reflections of our inherited traumas and the most significant opportunities for healing. Within the crucible of connection, we can confront and transform the legacies of the past, forging new patterns that will become the inheritance of those who follow.

The Role of Attachment and Relationships

In the intricate dance of human development, the earliest steps are often taken hand-in-hand with our primary caregivers. Within these formative relationships, the seeds of our future selves are sown, for better or worse. The attachment styles we develop as infants and children can become the templates for future relationships, influencing how we connect with others, manage emotional stress, and perceive the world around us. When these early bonds are disrupted by trauma, the reverberations can echo through generations.

Trauma, in its most insidious form, can infiltrate the nurturing bonds between parent and child. A parent's unresolved trauma can manifest as emotional unavailability, inconsistency, or even direct maltreatment. In their profound adaptability and need for attachment, children may internalize these patterns, misunderstanding them as reflections of their worth. They may grow to associate love with pain, care with unpredictability, and intimacy with danger. This internalized narrative can profoundly shape their emotional landscape, guiding them, often unconsciously, in their future relationships.

The transmission of trauma is not merely a psychological phenomenon. Still, it is also rooted in the biological processes that underpin our stress responses. When a child is exposed to a traumatic environment, their developing brain adapts to this heightened state of alert. These adaptations can be life-saving in the short term. Still, they may lead to long-term dysregulation of the body's stress response systems. Such dysregulation can leave an individual more vulnerable to mental health challenges. It can even influence the way they parent their children, thus perpetuating the cycle of trauma.

However, the story of attachment and relationships within the context of inherited family trauma is not one of deterministic gloom. It is also a testament to the resilience of the human spirit and the malleability of our relational blueprints. Secure attachments, whether formed in early childhood or developed through later reparative relationships, can offer a powerful counter-narrative to trauma. They can provide a sense of safety that allows for the exploration of vulnerability, the reevaluation of self-worth, and the gradual healing of old wounds.

Therapeutic interventions, supportive relationships, and sometimes even the simple passage of time can contribute to reshaping attachment styles. The recognition and processing of inherited trauma can lead to a conscious uncoupling from destructive patterns. This journey towards healing is not linear nor straightforward, but it is possible. It requires a compassionate understanding of one's history and an unwavering commitment to forging a different path.

As we navigate the complexities of our relationships, we must acknowledge the profound impact our earliest attachments have on our lives. By understanding the role of these attachments in the perpetuation of family trauma, we can begin to unravel the webs we have woven. Through this understanding, we can seek to create new patterns, not only for ourselves but for the generations that follow. In the next breath of our exploration, we will delve into the generational cycles of trauma, examining how repetition and variation play out across the tapestry of time.

Generational Cycles: Repetition and Variation

In the intricate dance of family dynamics, the steps are often choreographed by the silent music of the past. As we delve into the generational cycles of inherited family trauma, we observe a complex interplay of repetition and variation. This pattern is as revealing as it is enigmatic.

Trauma, by its very nature, is a rupture—a profound disruption in the fabric of one's experience of safety, connection, and identity. When such a rupture occurs, it does not heal with time alone. Instead, it often leaves an indelible mark, not just on the individual who experienced it but also on the tapestry of their lineage. This mark can manifest as a pattern of behavior, an emotional response, or even a physiological reaction, passed down through generations, sometimes subtly, sometimes with the force of a tidal wave.

The repetition in these generational cycles can be seen in the recurrence of specific traumas within a family. Abuse, neglect, addiction, and violence are among the many forms of suffering that can become a legacy, handed down as if they were a family heirloom. Children born into environments where these patterns are the norm may grow to replicate the behaviors and coping mechanisms they observed in their parents and grandparents. The repetition is not merely a mimicry; it is often an unconscious enactment of unresolved pain.

Yet, within these cycles, there is also variation. No two individuals experience trauma in precisely the same way. Thus, how trauma is expressed and carried forward can differ significantly. One sibling may internalize the trauma, leading to a life marked by depression and self-doubt. At the same time, another may externalize it, becoming aggressive or engaging in risky behaviors. These variations are influenced by many factors, including personality, resilience, social support, and even the unique combination of genes inherited from one's ancestors.

Understanding these cycles requires a deep empathy for how trauma can shape a life. It calls for an analytical eye that can discern patterns often hidden in plain sight, woven into the daily lives of those affected. It also demands recognizing the strength and resilience that can emerge from such hardship. Within these generational cycles, there is also the potential for healing and transformation.

As we consider the role of attachment and relationships in the previous section, we recognize that the bonds formed between parent and child can either perpetuate the cycle of trauma or become the crucible for its resolution. The quality of these relationships often dictates the trajectory of the cycle, determining whether the repetition of trauma will be a curse or a challenge to overcome.

The path to breaking these cycles is difficult, as it often involves confronting painful truths and challenging deeply ingrained behaviors. Yet, it is a path that holds the promise of liberation—not just for the individual but for the generations that follow. In the next section, we will explore the burden of silence and secrecy that often accompanies family trauma and how breaking this silence can be a decisive step toward healing.

The Burden of Silence and Secrecy

Within family history, threads of silence and secrecy often run deep, weaving patterns that are as complex as they are concealed. The burden of these unspoken legacies can weigh heavily on the shoulders of subsequent generations, manifesting in subtle and profound ways.

Silence, in the context of inherited family trauma, is not merely the absence of dialogue; it is a presence, a force that shapes the contours of family life. It can be a protective measure, a shield raised to guard against the pain of past experiences. Yet, this silence often comes at a cost. It can create a vacuum where understanding and empathy might otherwise flourish, leaving individuals to grapple with the shadows of trauma without the solace of shared recognition or the guidance of narrative.

Secrecy, too, serves as a coping mechanism, a barrier erected to keep the outside world at bay. It is the keeper of stories that are too painful, shameful, or feared to be exposed to the light of day. But secrecy can also be a source of isolation. This wall separates family members and their histories from each other. The secrets we keep are not inert; they have the power to shape identities, influence relationships, and dictate behaviors.

The consequences of this silence and secrecy are not confined to the emotional and psychological realm. They can ripple through the very fabric of family life, affecting communication, trust, and the ability to form healthy attachments. Children raised in the shadow of unspoken trauma may learn to read the unarticulated cues of their caregivers, becoming hyper-vigilant or emotionally guarded as a result. They may need to understand their origins and costs to carry these adaptive behaviors into adulthood.

Moreover, the burden of silence and secrecy can lead to disconnection from one's heritage. Without the stories that anchor us to our past, we can feel adrift, untethered from the lineage that has, in part, shaped who we are. This disconnection can be particularly disorienting in times of personal crisis when we most need a sense of continuity and belonging.

Yet, the silence is not impenetrable, nor is the secrecy absolute. Cracks can appear in the façade, often at unexpected moments:

- A family gathering.
- A comment made in passing.
- A reaction that seems disproportionate to its cause.

These fissures can provide glimpses into the hidden chambers of family history, offering opportunities for healing and understanding.

Breaking the silence and piercing the veil of secrecy requires courage. It demands a willingness to confront painful truths and to bear witness to the suffering of those who came before us. It also requires compassion for ourselves and our ancestors, whose choices were often dictated by circumstances beyond their control.

As we navigate the complexities of inherited family trauma, we must strive to balance the need for protection with the need for revelation. In doing so, we can begin to loosen the grip of the past and transform the burden of silence and secrecy into a legacy of resilience and openness. Through this transformation, we can forge new patterns in the webs we weave, patterns that honor our history without being trapped by it.

Trauma and Identity Formation

As we delve deeper into the intricate relationship between trauma and identity formation, it is essential to recognize that the impact of inherited family trauma is not merely a footnote in the story of an individual's life; it is often a central chapter that influences the narrative arc in profound ways. Identity, the sense of self that we carry and present to the world, is a mosaic of our experiences, beliefs, and the history that precedes us. When that history includes trauma, the pieces of the mosaic can take on different shades, sometimes darker and more complex than we might have anticipated.

For many, the realization that their identity has been partly shaped by the traumas of their forebears can be unsettling. It raises questions about autonomy and free will: How much of who I am is truly mine, and how much is the legacy of pain I carry within me? This is not to say that inherited trauma dictates one's destiny or diminishes the capacity for growth and self-determination. Instead, it suggests that the journey of self-discovery must also include a journey through the past, a process of understanding and, where possible, healing.

The imprints of trauma can manifest in various aspects of identity, including the roles we adopt within our families and communities, the values we hold dear, and the coping mechanisms we develop to navigate the world. A child raised in the shadow of a parent's unspoken grief may learn to tread lightly to avoid the landmines of emotion that seem to lurk beneath the surface. Another might internalize a sense of resilience, a legacy of ancestors who survived and persevered through unimaginable hardships.

Yet, the influence of trauma on identity is not always about the direct transmission of specific behaviors or attitudes. Sometimes, it is about the absence of specific experiences or expressions. The void left by a grandparent's untold story, the silence that shrouds a family's collective pain, can create a palpable presence in one's life, a blank space on the canvas of identity that begs to be acknowledged and understood.

In grappling with how inherited trauma shapes identity, it is crucial to approach the subject with compassion for oneself and one's lineage. The process of untangling the webs of trauma is not about assigning blame or dwelling in the realm of what-ifs. It is about recognizing the strength and vulnerability that coexist within the human spirit and the capacity to carry forward the wounds and the wisdom of those who came before us.

As we move forward in our exploration of inherited family trauma, we must hold space for the complexity of identity formation, for the interplay of light and shadow that defines our personal and collective histories. In doing so, we honor not only the struggles of our ancestors but also our ongoing journey toward understanding, healing, and, ultimately, transformation.

Chapter Summary

- Family histories can reveal patterns of trauma, such as war, abuse, or loss, that affect subsequent generations through behaviors and emotional responses.
- These patterns can be harmful, perpetuating pain cycles, and positive, inspiring resilience and determination.
- Empathy and critical analysis are needed to identify these patterns, understanding that memory and storytelling are subjective and influenced by cultural and personal biases.
- Recognizing familial patterns helps differentiate which emotional traits are inherited and which can be released to break cycles of trauma.
- Early attachment styles with caregivers set templates for future relationships. They can be disrupted by trauma, affecting stress management and perception.
- Trauma is transmitted through both psychological and biological processes, influencing parenting and perpetuating cycles, but secure attachments can counteract this.
- Generational cycles of trauma involve repetition of behaviors like abuse or neglect, but also variation, as individuals respond differently based on many factors.
- Silence and secrecy in families can perpetuate trauma, but breaking this silence can lead to healing and the creation of new, healthier patterns.

2

THE BODY KEEPS THE SCORE: PHYSIOLOGICAL IMPACTS

The Biology of Trauma

The biology of trauma is not confined to the psychological realm; it is deeply rooted in the very physiology of our bodies, influencing the complex interplay of genes, hormones, and neural pathways.

When we consider the physiological impacts of trauma, we must acknowledge the body's initial response mechanisms. These are the acute, often life-saving reactions that occur in the face of threat: the rapid heartbeat, adrenaline surge, and heightened senses. These responses are orchestrated by the sympathetic nervous system, which acts as a mobilizing force, preparing the body for action.

However, the effects of trauma extend beyond these immediate responses. When the body is subjected to chronic stress or repeated traumatic events, the stress response system can become dysregulated. Cortisol, a hormone released in response to stress, can be chronically elevated, or levels may become blunted over time. This dysregulation can lead to various physical health problems, such as increased susceptibility to illness, inflammation, and metabolic irregularities.

Moreover, trauma can leave its mark on the brain. Neuroimaging studies have shown that exposure to trauma can lead to changes in the structure and function of the brain, particularly in areas involved in processing emotions and memory, such as the amygdala, hippocampus, and prefrontal cortex. These alterations can affect an individual's ability to regulate emotions, create and retrieve memories, and respond to future stressors.

The enduring nature of these physiological changes raises a profound question: can the impact of trauma be passed down from one generation to the next? The burgeoning field of epigenetics provides a compelling answer. Epigenetic mechanisms, such as DNA methylation, can modify the expression of genes without altering the genetic code itself. These modifications can be influenced by environmental factors, including traumatic experiences, and, crucially, they can be inherited.

Thus, the legacy of trauma is not solely a narrative of psychological scars; it is also a biological reality. The children and grandchildren of those who have suffered may inherit a predisposition to specific stress responses, even in the absence of direct exposure to trauma. This inheritance can manifest as a heightened sensitivity to stress or an increased risk for various physical and mental health conditions.

It is within this biological framework that we begin to understand the profound and far-reaching consequences of inherited family trauma. The body keeps the score, recording the echoes of past traumas in the very cells and systems that sustain life. As we delve deeper into the science of stress responses across generations, we uncover not only the mechanisms of inheritance but also the potential for healing and resilience that can disrupt the cycle of trauma.

Stress Responses Across Generations

Like a sad melody that lingers in the air long after the last note has been played, the physiological impacts of trauma can reverberate through generations, subtly influencing the stress responses of descendants.

As we delve deeper into the physiological impacts of inherited family trauma, it becomes evident that the body does, indeed, keep the score. The stress responses that were once adaptive for our ancestors, enabling them to survive threats and dangers, may become maladaptive in their offspring, manifesting in heightened states of anxiety, vigilance, or fear even in the absence of direct threats.

These inherited stress responses are not merely psychological artifacts; they are deeply rooted in the very biology of the body. Children and grandchildren of those who have endured severe trauma may find themselves with a biological inheritance that primes them for a heightened stress response. This legacy is not one of choice and is not quickly shed.

The mechanisms through which these stress responses are passed down are complex and multifaceted. They involve the stories told and behaviors learned within a family and the silent, unseen transmission of physiological changes. These changes can alter how the body responds to stress, potentially affecting heart rate, cortisol levels, and even the structure and function of the brain.

The body's stress response system, primarily the hypothalamic-pituitary-adrenal (HPA) axis, can be tuned by early life experiences to become more reactive or more restrained. This tuning can be beneficial, preparing an individual to cope with the specific challenges of their environment. However, when the environment changes or the stress response is calibrated too high or too low, it can lead to a mismatch between the individual's physiological responses and the demands of their current context.

Moreover, the body's response to stress is not only about the immediate adrenaline surge or cortisol release. It is also about the long-term effects these responses have on the body. Chronic activation of the stress response system can lead to wear and tear on the body, a concept known as allostatic load. As emerging research suggests, this burden can accumulate over a lifetime. It may be passed on to the next generation, predisposing them to various health issues.

The implications of these findings are profound. They suggest that the work of healing from trauma is not only an individual pursuit but a generational one. It is a process that requires understanding, compassion, and a recognition of the invisible threads that connect the past, present, and future.

As we move forward, the conversation will shift to the burgeoning field of epigenetics, which offers a scientific framework for understanding how the effects of trauma can be transmitted across generations without direct changes to the DNA sequence. This field holds the promise of unraveling the complex interplay between genes and the environment, providing insights into how the legacy of trauma is carried within us and how we might begin to untangle its threads.

Epigenetics: The Interface of Genes and Environment

In the intricate dance of life, our genes choreograph a complex routine, not performed in isolation but in constant interaction with the environment. This interplay, a field known as epigenetics, reveals how external factors can influence the expression of our genes without altering the genetic code itself. It is within this nuanced biological conversation that we begin to understand how the echoes of inherited family trauma may reverberate through generations.

The concept of epigenetics bridges the once-wide chasm between nature and nurture. It suggests that our behaviors, experiences, and even our ancestors' experiences can leave a molecular mark on our DNA. These marks do not change the sequence of the DNA but can affect how cells "read" genes. This means that the legacy of trauma is not only psychological but can also be biological.

Consider a family tree with roots that delve deep into soils rich with history and strife. The branches of this tree may bear the unseen scars of past generations' adversities. When a grandparent experiences trauma, the stress can lead to chemical changes in their DNA. These changes, known as epigenetic modifications, can be passed down to their children and grandchildren, influencing their susceptibility to stress and mental health disorders.

The mechanism behind this transmission is not a direct handover of traumatic memories but rather an alteration in the stress response systems. For instance, the hypothalamic-pituitary-adrenal (HPA) axis, which regulates our stress response, can be modified epigenetically, leading to heightened or muted reactions to stress. These modifications can prime the body to react to threats in a way that may have been adaptive in a traumatic environment but can be maladaptive in a safe one.

Moreover, the nurturing environment provided by parents can also have epigenetic effects. A mother's care can lead to the development of a specific type of glucocorticoid receptor in her offspring, which helps them manage stress effectively. Conversely, a lack of nurturing care can result in fewer receptors, leading to a more sensitive stress response. This illustrates how the care we receive can shape our epigenetic makeup, potentially counteracting some of the inherited modifications.

The implications of epigenetic inheritance are profound, suggesting that the work of healing from trauma is not solely psychological or individual but can also be biological and collective. It opens up new avenues for understanding how interventions, such as therapy, social support, and lifestyle changes, might not only help individuals but also have the potential to break the cycle of transmitted trauma for future generations.

As we delve deeper into the physiological impacts of inherited family trauma, we must consider the body as a vessel that carries not just the genetic blueprint passed down from our ancestors but also the subtle imprints of their experiences. The body, in its wisdom, keeps the score. Through epigenetics, we begin to decipher the scoresheet, understanding the marks left by the past as we navigate the path toward healing.

Somatic Memory and the Trauma Landscape

In the intricate tapestry of human physiology, somatic memory stands out as a profound testament to the body's capacity to remember and, in some cases, relive experiences of trauma. This phenomenon extends beyond the individual, reaching back through generations, as the echoes of ancestral pain are not solely confined to the realm of narrative and lore but are also inscribed within the human fabric of their descendants.

In its wisdom, the body often becomes a repository for the unspoken, unresolved, and unfathomable traumas courting through the bloodlines. Though not directly experienced by the individual, these traumas can manifest as somatic symptoms—physical sensations, pains, or ailments for which there is no apparent cause. It is as if the body itself becomes a landscape, marked by the topography of inherited trauma, with each physical manifestation serving as a landmark to a past that is not entirely one's own.

This landscape is not uniform; it varies from person to person, shaped by the unique interplay of genetic predisposition and environmental factors. Some may carry the weight of this legacy in their posture, a particular stoop of the shoulders as if bearing an invisible burden. Others might experience inexplicable anxieties, a heart that races at the whisper of a memory that does not belong to them, or a sudden breathlessness as if the air of a bygone era has momentarily become too thick to breathe.

The science of psychoneuroimmunology has begun to unravel the complex communication network between the mind, the nervous system, and the immune system, suggesting that the body's physiological responses can indeed be influenced by psychological trauma. This communication network is not a one-way street; it is a dynamic, bidirectional flow of information that can perpetuate a state of heightened alertness or chronic stress, often without the individual's conscious awareness.

As we delve deeper into the somatic expressions of inherited trauma, it becomes increasingly clear that these are not merely psychological phenomena cloaked in physical form. They result from a profound entanglement of the emotional and the human, where the body serves as both a sensor and a scribe, recording the silent stories of past generations.

The implications of this understanding are vast, as they challenge the traditional boundaries between mind and body, between past and present. They call for a compassionate and holistic approach to healing, acknowledging the full spectrum of inheritance that shapes our being. It is a journey that requires us to listen intently to the whispers of our bodies, honor the legacy they carry, and engage in the delicate work of untangling the threads of trauma that are woven into our very flesh and blood.

As we move forward, the exploration of how these somatic memories translate into tangible health outcomes will further illuminate the enduring impact of ancestral trauma. It will guide us in finding pathways to understand and heal the wounds that time has not erased, fostering resilience and hope for future generations.

Health Outcomes Linked to Ancestral Trauma

Research has begun to shed light on how the echoes of our forebears' hardships reverberate through time, leaving biological imprints on their descendants. Epigenetics, the study of how genes can be turned on or off by environmental factors, has provided a framework for understanding how the stress and trauma experienced by one generation can alter the genetic expression of the next. These changes do not alter the DNA sequence. Still, they can influence how genes are expressed, potentially predisposing individuals to various health conditions.

For instance, studies have shown that the children and grandchildren of individuals who have endured extreme stress, such as survivors of the Holocaust or famine, may have an increased risk for specific health issues, including metabolic disorders and mental health conditions. This suggests that the physiological stress responses shaped by trauma can be passed down, potentially priming the body to react more intensely to stressors or disrupting normal metabolic processes.

Moreover, the impact of inherited family trauma is not limited to direct physiological effects. It can also influence behaviors that contribute to health outcomes. For example, a family history of trauma may lead to patterns of coping that include substance abuse, overeating, or avoidance, which can, in turn, lead to a host of chronic health conditions, such as heart disease, obesity, and addiction.

The implications of these findings are profound, as they suggest that an individual's health cannot be fully understood without considering the historical context of their lineage. The experiences of our ancestors are inscribed in the very fabric of our being, influencing not only our susceptibility to certain diseases but also our resilience in the face of new challenges.

As we continue to unravel the mysteries of how ancestral trauma affects health, it becomes increasingly clear that the care we provide must be holistic, acknowledging the intricate interplay between our genetic heritage, our personal experiences, and the environment in which we live. It is a call to look beyond the individual to the ancestral stories that shape our health narratives and to approach healing with a compassionate and scientifically informed understanding.

In this light, the journey toward wellness becomes a personal quest and a collective endeavor to heal the wounds of the past so that future generations may be freed from the physiological burdens of unspoken histories. The body, indeed, keeps the score. Still, through awareness, research, and empathy, we can begin to settle the accounts of the past and chart a path toward a healthier future.

Chapter Summary

- The biology of trauma affects our genes, hormones, and neural pathways, with effects that can span generations.
- Trauma triggers an acute stress response orchestrated by the sympathetic nervous system, preparing the body for action.
- Chronic stress or repeated trauma can lead to dysregulation of the stress response system, causing physical health problems.
- Trauma can alter brain structures like the amygdala, hippocampus, and prefrontal cortex, affecting emotion regulation and memory.
- Epigenetics shows that trauma can lead to inheritable changes in gene expression without altering the DNA sequence itself.
- The physiological changes from trauma, including altered stress responses, can be passed down, affecting descendants' health and stress sensitivity.
- The field of epigenetics bridges nature and nurture, suggesting that experiences can leave molecular marks on DNA that influence gene expression.
- Ancestral trauma can manifest as somatic symptoms and influence health outcomes, necessitating a holistic approach to healing that considers generational impacts.

3

IN THE MIND'S EYE: PSYCHOLOGICAL CONSEQUENCES

The Psychological Imprint of Trauma

Trauma, by its very nature, is a complex beast, often casting long shadows not only over the life of the one who directly experiences it but also across the generations that follow. The psychological imprint of trauma is a profound and pervasive mark that can shape the mental landscape of descendants in ways that are both subtle and significant.

To understand the impact of inherited family trauma, it is essential to recognize that the transmission of trauma is not merely a matter of narrative inheritance, where stories of past hardships are passed down through the family lore. Instead, it is a more insidious process that can alter the very fabric of an individual's psychological makeup. This alteration can manifest in various forms, including heightened anxiety and depression, which we will explore in greater depth.

Anxiety, a state of heightened apprehension and fear, is often a typical response to trauma. When trauma is inherited, this anxiety can become a baseline state for those who carry the legacy of their forebears' suffering. It may present as a pervasive sense of unease, a constant anticipation of threat, or an inability to find comfort in the predictability of daily life. For some, this anxiety is diffuse, lacking an explicit source or trigger, making it all the more challenging to address and manage.

Depression, on the other hand, can be seen as the heavy cloak of inherited trauma. It can weigh down individuals with a sense of hopelessness, a loss of interest in life, and a pervasive sadness that seems to have no beginning or end. This form of depression is not simply a reaction to one's immediate circumstances. Still, it is often a more profound, more existential despair that echoes previous generations' unresolved grief and losses.

The mechanisms through which these psychological states are transmitted are varied and complex. They may involve behavioral patterns modeled by traumatized parents, biochemical changes resulting from stress, or even epigenetic modifications that alter how genes are expressed without changing the genetic code. These epigenetic changes can then be passed down, potentially predisposing offspring to similar psychological struggles.

It is crucial to acknowledge that the inheritance of trauma is not a destiny set in stone. Resilience, too, can be a family legacy. The recognition of these patterns is the first step toward healing. With appropriate support and intervention, individuals can learn to navigate their inherited landscapes of anxiety and depression. Through therapy, mindfulness practices, and sometimes medication, the chains of trauma can be loosened, allowing for a reclamation of agency and a path toward a more hopeful future.

As we delve further into the nuances of inherited family trauma, we will explore not only the challenges it presents but also the opportunities for growth and transformation that can arise when these deep-seated psychological imprints are brought into the light of conscious awareness.

Anxiety, Depression, and Inherited Trauma

In the labyrinth of the human psyche, the shadows of anxiety and depression often lurk, hidden yet potent. When these shadows are cast by one's own experiences and the silent legacy of ancestral pain, their grip can be particularly tenacious. Inherited family trauma, a phenomenon only recently gaining broader recognition within the psychological community, can manifest as a predisposition to these debilitating mental health conditions.

Anxiety, a state of heightened apprehension and fear, is a natural stress response. However, when this response is magnified or triggered by seemingly innocuous events, it may echo past family traumas. Individuals carrying this burden may find themselves inexplicably tense, their bodies bracing for threats that are no longer present, their minds trapped by a history they may not fully comprehend.

Similarly, depression can be a heavy cloak woven from threads of sadness, hopelessness, and fatigue. It can descend upon a person with a weight that feels both inexplicably personal and eerily foreign. For those with inherited trauma, depression may not always arise from their immediate life circumstances. Still, it may be an emotional resonance from ancestral struggles, losses, or hardships that were never fully processed or healed.

The mechanisms through which these conditions are passed down are complex and multifaceted. Epigenetics, the study of how genes can be turned on or off by environmental factors, suggests that our forebears' experiences can shape our genes' expression, potentially predisposing us to similar psychological states. Moreover, the family environment, with its patterns of behavior, communication, and emotional expression, can perpetuate a legacy of anxiety and depression, teaching new generations to respond to the world in ways that mirror the unresolved traumas of the past.

It is crucial to acknowledge that while the inheritance of trauma can predispose individuals to anxiety and depression, it does not dictate destiny. The human mind possesses a remarkable capacity for resilience and healing. Understanding the origins of one's emotional landscape can be a decisive first step in the journey toward recovery. This knowledge can illuminate the path for therapeutic interventions that address the individual's current symptoms and honor and heal the wounds carried from generations past.

As we delve deeper into the psychological consequences of inherited family trauma, we must also consider the cognitive dimensions of this legacy. How thought patterns and beliefs are shaped by the silent narratives of our ancestors' experiences can profoundly influence our perceptions and reactions to the world around us. Within this intricate interplay of past and present, memory and experience, we find the keys to unlocking the patterns that bind us and the potential for transformation that lies within.

Cognitive Echoes: Thought Patterns and Beliefs

In the labyrinthine corridors of the mind, where memories and experiences intertwine, the legacy of inherited family trauma often manifests as persistent cognitive echoes that shape thought patterns and beliefs. These echoes reverberate through generations, subtly influencing the mental frameworks within which individuals operate. The psychological consequences of such inherited trauma are not merely emotional but also cognitive, affecting how one perceives the world and oneself.

The insidious nature of these cognitive echoes lies in their ability to operate below the level of conscious awareness. Individuals may find themselves harboring beliefs that are not the product of their own experiences but are instead inherited remnants of their ancestors' unprocessed traumas. These beliefs can manifest in various ways, such as a pervasive sense of danger in safe situations, an underlying feeling of unworthiness, or a tendency to expect abandonment or betrayal without cause.

Thought patterns, too, can be shaped by these inherited echoes. A person might be prone to catastrophic thinking, always anticipating the worst outcome, because their forebears lived through times when such outcomes were expected. Alternatively, one might engage in black-and-white thinking, struggling to see the nuances in situations or people, mirroring the survival mechanisms of ancestors who lived when quick, decisive judgments were necessary.

The impact of these thought patterns and beliefs is profound. They can influence one's choices and behaviors, often leading to self-fulfilling prophecies that reinforce the inherited trauma narrative. For instance, a belief in inevitable abandonment can lead to behaviors that push others away, thus perpetuating a cycle of isolation and reinforcing the belief.

Recognizing and addressing these cognitive echoes is a crucial step in healing from inherited family trauma. It requires a deep and often challenging introspection to discern which aspects of one's thought patterns and beliefs are genuinely personal and which are echoes of the past. Therapeutic interventions, such as cognitive-behavioral therapy, narrative therapy, or family systems therapy, can provide the tools to untangle these inherited threads.

Through this process, individuals can begin to rewrite the cognitive scripts handed down to them, crafting beliefs and thought patterns more congruent with their own experiences and aspirations. As they do so, they not only liberate themselves from the weight of their ancestors' unprocessed traumas but also halt the transmission of these psychological patterns to future generations.

The journey of healing from inherited family trauma is not a solitary one. It is a collective endeavor that requires compassion, understanding, and the courage to confront the shadows that linger in the mind's eye. By doing so, one can emerge with a newfound sense of agency and the ability to craft a narrative that honors the past without being trapped.

The Shadow of Trauma in Dreams and Imagination

In the quiet solitude of the night, when the conscious mind slips into the background, the subconscious takes the stage. It is here, in the realm of dreams and imagination, that the shadow of inherited family trauma often manifests most vividly. The individuals carrying this legacy may find themselves haunted by recurring nightmares or besieged by intrusive thoughts that seem to arise from a well of collective memory rather than personal experience.

In their enigmatic language, dreams often serve as the canvas upon which these inherited fears and anxieties are painted. A grandchild of war refugees might dream of fleeing an unseen enemy, the emotional residue of their grandparents' harrowing escapes embedded within their psyche. These nocturnal visions, while abstract, carry the emotional weight of the original trauma, suggesting that the experiences of our ancestors can indeed ripple through generations, influencing the deepest layers of our minds.

The imagination, too, can be a fertile ground for these inherited narratives to take root. It is not uncommon for individuals to find themselves drawn to specific themes in literature or cinema that resonate with their family's past traumas. They may feel a profound connection to stories of loss and survival without fully understanding why. This inexplicable pull towards certain narratives can be a subconscious attempt to make sense of the echoes of trauma that reside within them.

The interplay between dreams and imagination in the context of inherited family trauma is complex. Both can act as a mirror reflecting previous generations' unresolved emotions and experiences. Yet, they also provide a means for expression and processing. Through dreams, the mind attempts to reconcile the past's unresolved conflicts. At the same time, the imagination offers a space to explore and understand these inherited emotional landscapes.

It is crucial to recognize that these psychological phenomena are not merely echoes of a bygone era but are active elements in the individual's current emotional life. They can shape one's perception of the world, influence relationships, and even guide life choices. Acknowledging the presence of these inherited patterns is the first step towards understanding their impact and integrating them into one's narrative to foster growth and healing.

As we delve deeper into the psychological consequences of inherited family trauma, we begin to see that the mind's eye—through dreams and imagination—does not merely reflect past sorrows but also holds the potential for resilience and transformation. Within this inner landscape, the seeds of coping mechanisms and the capacity for resilience are sown, allowing individuals to navigate the complexities of their inherited stories with strength and grace.

Coping Mechanisms and Resilience

As we delve deeper into the psychological landscape shaped by inherited family trauma, we find that individuals are not merely passive recipients of their ancestors' legacies. Instead, they are active participants in their psychological journey, often employing a variety of coping mechanisms to navigate the complex emotional terrain they have inherited. While diverse in form and function, these mechanisms serve as a testament to human resilience in the face of intergenerational pain.

Coping mechanisms can be as unique as the individuals who deploy them, tailored to their specific needs and circumstances. Some may find solace in the arts, using creative expression to process and externalize the emotions that simmer beneath the surface. Writing, painting, and music become conduits for unspoken feelings, releasing tension that might otherwise remain trapped within the psyche.

Others may turn to the structure and support of rituals and traditions. Often passed down through generations, these practices can provide a sense of continuity and belonging that counteracts the isolation trauma can engender. By engaging in these time-honored customs, individuals can connect with their ancestors in a way that is both healing and empowering, drawing strength from the very roots that once seemed to tether them to their familial pain.

Social support systems also play a critical role in the resilience of those dealing with inherited trauma. The presence of empathetic friends, family members, or even professional therapists can provide a reflective surface for one's experiences. In the presence of a compassionate other, an individual can begin to untangle the complex web of emotions and begin the process of understanding and integrating their trauma.

Mindfulness and meditation have also emerged as powerful tools for those grappling with the echoes of ancestral suffering. These practices encourage a presence of mind that can help to quiet the tumultuous inner dialogue that trauma can provoke. By fostering a sense of calm and centeredness, mindfulness can help individuals approach their inherited challenges with a clearer perspective, making it possible to respond rather than react to the emotional triggers they encounter.

Physical activity and connection to the body are equally important. Trauma can often lead to a disconnection from one's physical self. Still, activities such as yoga, dance, or even simple exercise can help to bridge that gap. By becoming attuned to the sensations and needs of their bodies, individuals can reclaim a sense of agency and vitality that trauma may have diminished.

It is important to note that coping mechanisms are not a one-size-fits-all solution. What offers profound relief to one person may not resonate with another. The key is the exploration and the willingness to engage with various strategies to discover what best facilitates one's journey toward healing.

Moreover, resilience should not be mistaken for a lack of vulnerability. It is not the absence of pain or struggle but rather the capacity to persevere despite it. Resilience is the courage to confront the darkest chapters of one's family history and seek the light that can lead to a more hopeful narrative for future generations.

In this ongoing process, individuals may find that their coping mechanisms evolve. As they grow and change, so do their needs and strategies for meeting them. This evolution is a natural part of the healing journey. It is a sign that the individual is not static but is instead moving forward, ever adapting to the contours of their inherited landscape.

The resilience of those who face inherited family trauma is a profound reminder of the human capacity for growth and transformation. It is a testament to the strength that can emerge when one faces the past with courage and the future with hope.

Chapter Summary

- Trauma has long-lasting psychological effects that can affect not just the individual but also their descendants, altering their mental health.
- Inherited trauma can lead to heightened anxiety and depression, presenting as a constant sense of unease or profound existential despair.
- Transmission of trauma can occur through behavioral modeling, biochemical changes due to stress, and epigenetic modifications that affect gene expression.
- Recognizing inherited trauma patterns is the first step toward healing, with therapy, mindfulness, and medication as potential aids.
- Inherited family trauma can predispose individuals to anxiety and depression, but understanding and therapeutic intervention can foster resilience and recovery.
- Cognitive echoes from inherited trauma can shape thought patterns and beliefs, influencing perceptions and reactions to the world.

- Dreams and imagination can vividly reflect inherited trauma, with recurring nightmares and themes that resonate with ancestral experiences.
- Coping mechanisms and resilience are vital to navigating inherited trauma, with creative expression, rituals, social support, mindfulness, and physical activity as helpful strategies.

4

THE LANGUAGE OF TRAUMA: COMMUNICATION AND EXPRESSION

Narratives of Pain: Storytelling and Memory

In the realm of inherited family trauma, the stories that are passed down from generation to generation carry with them not only the explicit narratives of our ancestors' experiences but also the implicit emotional residue of their pain. These narratives of pain, woven into the very fabric of family history, are often recounted through storytelling and the shared memory of the collective.

In this context, storytelling serves as a powerful vessel for transmitting trauma. It is a means by which experiences are given a voice, allowing for the externalization of internal suffering. Recounting one's story, or the stories of those before us, is not merely a recitation of facts; it is an emotional journey that can rekindle the smoldering embers of past anguish.

Memory plays a pivotal role in this process. It is selective, often highlighting the most traumatic events, and through this lens, the past is remembered and conveyed. The stories told are rarely neutral; they are colored by the emotions they evoke in the teller and the listener. Though personal, these memories become shared artifacts within the family, shaping future generations' identity and emotional landscape.

The power of these narratives lies not only in the words spoken but also in the silences between them. It is within these silences that the unspeakable is often housed. The things too painful to articulate, the experiences that words fail to capture, reside in the quiet moments that punctuate the storytelling. These silences speak volumes, conveying the depth of trauma that can be too overwhelming to express verbally.

As these stories are told and retold, they are not static; they evolve with each iteration, influenced by the narrator's current emotional state and understanding. How a story is told at one moment may differ from its recounting years later as insights are gained and perspectives shift. This fluidity allows for a dynamic engagement with the past, which can be healing and potentially retraumatizing.

The act of storytelling within the context of inherited family trauma is not merely about preserving history; it is about grappling with the emotional inheritance that accompanies that history. It is a process through which understanding can be sought and, perhaps, a measure of peace can be found. Through the narratives of pain, individuals and families engage in a complex dance with their past, attempting to find a way to integrate these stories into their lives without being consumed by them.

In the ongoing journey to comprehend and mitigate the effects of inherited trauma, it is essential to recognize the profound impact that storytelling and memory have on individuals and the collective family psyche. By giving voice to the pain of the past, there is hope for a future where the weight of this inheritance can be acknowledged, understood, and transformed with time and effort.

Nonverbal Transmission: Gestures, Posture, and Silence

Inherited family trauma often weaves itself into the fabric of our being, not only through the stories told but also through the silent language of our bodies. The way we carry ourselves, the gestures we make, and the silences we hold can be powerful communicators of the experiences that have shaped us, often without our conscious awareness.

Gestures, those subtle or pronounced movements we make with our hands, faces, or bodies, can be echoes of past traumas. A clenched fist, a furrowed brow, or a chronic avoidance of eye contact might be the physical manifestations of emotional pain passed down through generations. These gestures can become a part of a family's behavioral vocabulary, a nonverbal lexicon of shared suffering.

Posture, too, tells its own story. The way one might slump their shoulders, protectively hunch over, or hold tension in the neck can be indicative of internalized trauma. It's as if the body remembers what the mind tries to forget, and it expresses this memory in a language all its own. The body's posture can be a reservoir for anxiety, fear, and the weight of unspoken stories that have been inherited from those who came before.

Silence, in the context of inherited family trauma, is particularly poignant. It is not merely the absence of sound but a presence filled with unarticulated emotions and untold stories. It can be a heavy blanket under which the unspeakable is hidden or a protective space where healing begins. The silence of a family can be a powerful transmitter of trauma, as what is not said is often as influential as what is spoken aloud. It can be a learned response, a way of coping passed down, teaching each generation to internalize their pain and communicate through a quiet language of shared understanding.

The nonverbal cues we inherit and perpetuate within our families are not always negative. They can also be a source of strength and resilience. A gentle touch, a warm embrace, or a steady, supportive stance can be nonverbal affirmations of love and solidarity that have helped previous generations endure and can provide a foundation of support for the present.

Understanding the nonverbal transmission of inherited family trauma requires a keen sense of observation and a deep empathy for how these unspoken elements can influence our lives. Only by recognizing and acknowledging these silent communicators can we begin to address the trauma they represent and transform them into expressions of healing and growth. As we move forward, we find that the arts and creative expression offer a powerful avenue for this transformation, providing a voice to the voiceless gestures, postures, and silences that have shaped our existence.

Artistic and Creative Outlets

In the realm of inherited family trauma, where words often fall short, and silence can be deafening, individuals may find solace and expression through the universal language of art. Artistic and creative outlets serve as a conduit for the emotions and experiences that are otherwise inexpressible in the traditional lexicon of trauma discourse.

The canvas becomes a silent witness to the internal turmoil, the paintbrush a tool to navigate the labyrinth of generational pain. Through strokes and colors, the artist communicates the nuances of their inherited sorrow, often revealing insights previously obscured by the limitations of verbal language. Creating art is not merely a form of self-expression; it is a dialogue with the past, a way of understanding and integrating the experiences woven into the fabric of one's lineage.

Similarly, the written word, though paradoxically part of the language system, can transcend its boundaries through poetry and narrative. The rhythm and flow of poetry allow for an abstraction and distillation of emotions, capturing the essence of trauma in a personal and universal way. On the other hand, narrative writing can be a systematic excavation of family history, a way to give voice to the stories that have been silenced, and a means to reconstruct a fragmented identity.

Music, with its melodies and harmonies, resonates with the unspeakable elements of our shared human experience. It can evoke the deepest of emotions and memories, often serving as a bridge between the present and the past, between what is said and what is felt. Music can be a healing force for those with inherited trauma. This vibrational companion understands without judgment.

Dance and movement therapy offers another dimension of expression. The body, which often bears the bodily imprint of trauma, finds its language through movement, releasing the stories etched in muscle and sinew. Inherited patterns of tension and holding can be explored and, with time, transformed into movements of liberation and resilience.

These artistic and creative outlets offer a means of communication and a path to healing. They allow for a reclamation of agency, providing a space where one can safely explore and reshape the narrative of their inherited trauma. Through these practices, individuals can begin to untangle the threads of their family's past, weaving a new tapestry of understanding and meaning that honors their history while forging a new way forward.

In embracing the arts as a form of expression, we acknowledge the complexity of human emotion and how trauma can shape, but not define, our existence. In the act of creation, it is here that the language of trauma finds its most profound and eloquent voice.

The Role of Language in Shaping Experience

Language is not merely a tool for communication; it is the architecture of our inner world, the framework through which we construct reality and give shape to our experiences. In the realm of inherited family trauma, language becomes a vessel that carries the weight of past generations, often without our conscious awareness. Through language, unspoken pains are hinted at, and through language, the unspeakable is sometimes inadvertently revealed.

How families communicate about trauma—or choose to remain silent—can significantly influence how individuals understand and internalize their ancestral past. The absence of language, the voids where stories should reside, can be as telling as the stories themselves. Silence can be a heavy burden, suggesting that some truths are too painful to articulate or that they must be cloistered away to protect the family's fabric. Yet, this silence can create an undercurrent of anxiety, a sense that there are obscured pieces of one's identity, fragments of a puzzle that one is not permitted to assemble.

Conversely, the presence of language can be equally potent. The words chosen to describe past traumas can color the emotional landscape of future generations. A family that speaks of its past with bitterness and resentment may inadvertently instill a sense of victimhood and anger in its descendants. On the other hand, narratives that emphasize resilience and survival can imbue a sense of strength and hope. The language used to convey these stories is not neutral; it is imbued with the power to shape perceptions, beliefs, and emotional responses.

Moreover, the metaphors and analogies employed to describe inherited trauma can either illuminate or obscure our understanding. When we use warlike metaphors, for example, we may adopt a combative stance towards our inherited pain, viewing it as an enemy to be defeated. Let's speak of trauma as a journey. We might instead see ourselves as travelers navigating a landscape that requires understanding and exploration. The choice of metaphor is not merely stylistic; it is a cognitive framing that can alter our approach to healing and self-awareness.

Language also plays a critical role in the intergenerational transmission of trauma. Research has shown that the narratives parents share with their children can either perpetuate a cycle of trauma or contribute to its resolution. When stories are shared with care and consciousness, acknowledging the pain while also encapsulating the lessons and growth that emerged from it, they can help the next generation contextualize and integrate these experiences into their lives healthily.

In essence, the role of language in shaping experience is profound. Through language, we encode and perpetuate our familial narratives. Through language, we have the opportunity to reframe and transform them. As we move forward, it becomes essential to consider how we can use language to convey inherited trauma and foster healing and growth. By cultivating new dialogues that honor the past while rewriting the trauma narrative, we can break the cycle and chart a course toward collective healing.

Breaking the Cycle: New Dialogues

In the intricate weave of human existence, the threads of trauma are often woven so intricately into the fabric of our family histories that they become almost indistinguishable from the patterns of daily life. The language we use to communicate our experiences, as explored in the preceding discussion, not only reflects but also reinforces the enduring impact of these traumas. Here, in the realm of expression, we find the potential to unravel these threads and weave a new narrative. This section delves into the transformative power of creating new dialogues to break the cycle of inherited family trauma.

The journey of healing is not embarked upon in silence. It requires the courage to speak and the strength to listen. New dialogues begin with acknowledging the past, not as a place of residence but as a point of reference. It is essential to recognize the patterns of communication that have perpetuated trauma, to understand the unspoken rules that have governed family interactions, and to bring them into the light of conscious discourse.

Breaking the cycle necessitates a language that moves beyond the confines of blame, shame, and guilt. It requires a lexicon of compassion, empathy, and understanding. Families must learn to articulate their pain without fearing judgment or retribution. This involves cultivating a space where vulnerability is not equated with weakness, but rather seen as a profound act of bravery. In this space, individuals are encouraged to express their emotions, share their stories, and articulate their needs.

One of the most significant shifts in dialogue comes from the transition from passive to active language. Rather than speaking about trauma as something that merely happens to an individual or family, it is empowering to discuss the active steps being taken to heal and grow. This shift in language reflects a shift in agency, from being victims of circumstance to being architects of one's healing journey.

Moreover, new dialogues involve the interweaving of multiple perspectives. Inherited family trauma is not a monolith; it affects each member differently. Creating a multifaceted conversation that honors each person's unique experiences is crucial. This means actively listening to one another, asking open-ended questions, and resisting the urge to impose one's narrative onto someone else's experience.

It is also essential to integrate new forms of communication that may have yet to be present. For some, this may mean exploring nonverbal forms of expression such as art, music, or movement, which can serve as powerful conduits for emotions that words cannot capture. For others, it may involve learning to set boundaries and assertively communicate one's limits, a skill often eroded in environments where trauma has dictated interactions.

In breaking the cycle of inherited family trauma, we are not merely altering the way we speak; we are transforming the way we connect with ourselves. This transformation is not instantaneous. It is a process that unfolds through consistent effort, patience, and a willingness to embrace the discomfort of change. Each new dialogue is a step towards a future where the legacy of trauma is not one of pain and silence but one of healing and growth.

As we continue to explore the language of trauma and its expression, it becomes evident that the power to redefine our experiences lies within our grasp. Through new dialogues, we can begin to untangle the knots of the past and weave a narrative that supports resilience, fosters understanding, and celebrates the possibility of renewal.

Chapter Summary

- Family trauma is passed down through stories that carry emotional pain, affecting future generations.
- Storytelling allows for the externalization of internal suffering and can rekindle past anguish.
- Memory selectively highlights traumatic events, shaping identity and emotional responses within families.
- The unspeakable aspects of trauma often reside in the silences between stories, conveying the depth of pain.
- Stories evolve, influenced by the narrator's emotions and understanding, which can be healing or retraumatizing.
- Storytelling is a way to grapple with emotional inheritance and seek understanding and peace.
- Recognizing the impact of storytelling and memory is crucial in comprehending and mitigating inherited trauma.
- Artistic and creative outlets provide a means to express and heal from trauma that words cannot fully capture.

5

THE TIES THAT BIND: FAMILY DYNAMICS

Roles and Expectations within the Family System

Within family dynamics, each member often finds themselves cast in roles that are as defining as they are limiting. These roles, shaped by the expectations of the family unit, can be both a source of comfort and a catalyst for perpetuating inherited trauma. As we delve into the nuances of these roles and expectations, we must consider how they contribute to the complex tapestry of intergenerational narratives.

Roles within the family are frequently assigned early in life, often without conscious intent. The eldest child may become the 'responsible one,' shouldering burdens that exceed their years. At the same time, the youngest might be labeled the 'baby,' perpetually seen as needing protection. While seemingly benign, these roles can set the stage for a lifetime of scripted behavior that stifles individual growth and perpetuates familial patterns.

Expectations, too, are woven into the fabric of family life. They can be explicit, such as the anticipation that children will follow in their parent's footsteps, or implicit, like the unspoken belief that one must never show weakness or vulnerability. These expectations often arise from the family's collective experiences and traumas, handed down like heirlooms, sometimes treasured, other times borne out of obligation.

These roles and expectations can be heavy, mainly when they are at odds with a person's authentic self. A child who yearns for artistic expression may be constrained by the expectation to pursue a more 'practical' profession. Another might struggle with the role of peacemaker, suppressing their needs to maintain fragile family harmony. In such ways, the family system, while providing a sense of identity and belonging, can also inadvertently trap members in cycles of trauma and unfulfillment.

By recognizing these roles and expectations, individuals can begin to understand the origins of their pain and those who came before them—acknowledging that these roles are not fixed but rather malleable narratives that allow for the possibility of change. By challenging and reshaping these expectations, family members can start to heal from inherited trauma, crafting new roles that align with their true selves and fostering a family dynamic that supports individuality and growth.

As we transition from exploring roles and expectations, we must consider the concepts of enmeshment and differentiation. These psychological constructs further illuminate how family members can become entangled in each other's lives, sometimes to the detriment of their individual development. Understanding the delicate balance between closeness and autonomy within the family system is crucial in addressing the complex interplay of inherited family trauma.

Enmeshment and Differentiation

When discussing family dynamics, the concepts of enmeshment and differentiation stand out as pivotal elements that shape the relational patterns and, consequently, the transmission of trauma from one generation to the next. These two forces act as the yin and yang within family systems, each holding the potential to foster healthy relationships or perpetuate cycles of inherited trauma.

Enmeshment, a term that may evoke the image of threads too tightly woven together, refers to relationships where personal boundaries are diffused, individuality is diminished, and emotional autonomy is scarce. In an enmeshed family, members may feel a heightened responsibility for each other's emotional states and decisions, often leading to a loss of personal identity. The intentions behind such closeness can be rooted in love and the desire for unity. Still, when taken to the extreme, it can create an environment where the individual's emotional well-being is inextricably tied to the family's collective psyche.

This lack of boundaries can mean that trauma is not an isolated experience; instead, it becomes a shared burden, passed down through the generations as quickly as heirlooms or genetic traits. When one member of the family experiences trauma, the emotional fallout can ripple through the enmeshed network, leaving each person to carry a piece of the pain, often without the tools or understanding to process it independently.

Differentiation, on the other hand, offers a contrasting approach to family relationships. It is the process by which individuals within the family system develop a strong sense of self while remaining connected to their loved ones. Differentiation allows members to express their thoughts, feelings, and desires without fear of losing emotional support or family ties. It is the balance between autonomy and intimacy, where family members can support one another without sacrificing individuality.

In a differentiated family, trauma may still occur. Still, its legacy is less likely to be woven into the fabric of the family's collective identity. Members are better equipped to offer support without becoming entangled in the trauma. They can acknowledge the pain of the past and work towards healing without allowing it to define them or their relationships.

The journey from enmeshment to differentiation is a complex one. It requires a conscious effort to establish healthy boundaries and a willingness to confront and understand the trauma that has been inherited. It is a delicate dance between honoring the interconnectedness of the family and nurturing the individual's right to a separate, autonomous existence.

As we explore family dynamics, it is essential to recognize the role that scapegoating can play within these relational patterns. Often, when the balance between enmeshment and differentiation is lost, families may unconsciously assign the role of the scapegoat to one member, who then becomes the depository for the family's unresolved issues and trauma. Understanding this dynamic is crucial in unraveling the complex tapestry of inherited family trauma and in paving the way for healing and transformation.

Scapegoating and the Family Scapegoat

Within the complex network of family relationships, a role is as enduring as it is damaging—the family scapegoat. Often unwittingly appointed, this individual bears the brunt of the family's collective dysfunction, carrying the weight of blame for problems far beyond their control. The scapegoating process is not just a matter of assigning fault in times of conflict; it is a complex mechanism that can perpetuate inherited family trauma across generations.

To understand the phenomenon of scapegoating, one must first recognize its roots in the family's unconscious effort to manage pain and disavow internal conflict. When a family system is unable to confront and process its traumas—be they rooted in abuse, neglect, addiction, or other forms of emotional turmoil—it may unconsciously designate one member to symbolize these unresolved issues. This person becomes the repository for the family's unspoken grief, anger, and shame.

The role of the scapegoat is often solidified in childhood and can be alarmingly stable over time. A child who exhibits vulnerability or reacts strongly to the family's dysfunction may be more likely to be cast in this role. Once established, the scapegoat becomes the focal point for criticism, with their actions and behaviors subjected to disproportionate scrutiny. This dynamic can severely impact the individual's self-esteem, relationships, and overall mental health.

The scapegoat's journey is one of profound isolation. They are frequently misunderstood and marginalized, not only within the family but also in their interactions with the world at large. The internalized belief that they are inherently flawed or responsible for the family's distress can lead to a self-fulfilling prophecy, where the scapegoat struggles with personal and professional relationships, reinforcing the family's narrative.

Yet, the role of the scapegoat is not without its paradoxes. While they are burdened with blame, they are also often the member who is most aware of the family's toxic patterns. Their unique position can grant them the insight and motivation to seek change for themselves and their family. It is not uncommon for the scapegoat to be the first to seek therapy or to break the cycle of trauma by refusing to participate in the dysfunctional family script.

The healing process for a family scapegoat involves a deep and often painful reevaluation of their place within the family narrative. It requires dismantling long-held beliefs and recreating a self-identity eroded by years of misplaced blame. Through therapeutic interventions, support systems, and personal resilience, the scapegoat can begin to shed the burdens that were never theirs to carry and forge a path toward a healthier, autonomous life.

The journey of the scapegoat is symbolic of the broader struggles within a family grappling with inherited trauma. It is a role that illuminates how pain, if left unaddressed, can warp the bonds meant to offer support and love. In recognizing the dynamics of scapegoating, families can begin to untangle the threads of their shared history, confront the traumas that bind them, and move toward a future where each member is seen, heard, and valued for who they are.

Secrets, Lies, and Family Myths

Within the complex interplay of family interactions, secrets, and lies often serve as the silent architects of dysfunction, shaping the emotional landscape of generations. Like specters in the family narrative, these hidden truths cast long shadows over descendants' lives, often without their conscious awareness. The myths that families construct around these secrets become the bedrock of inherited trauma, a legacy passed down as indeed as genetic traits.

The power of secrets lies not only in the content of what is hidden but also in the act of concealment itself. When a family chooses to bury the truth, it inadvertently creates an environment where reality is malleable, and trust becomes a casualty. Children raised in such families may develop a keen sense of vigilance, an unconscious radar for the unspoken or the unseen. They learn to read between the lines, to listen for the silences that speak volumes. This hypervigilance, while adaptive in the context of uncertainty, can become a burden, a predisposition to anxiety that haunts relationships and personal development.

Lies, whether by omission or commission, weave a complex tapestry of alternate reality. Family members may play roles in a story that feels inauthentic, a narrative that doesn't align with their inner experience. The dissonance between the outward family myth and the internal sense of truth can lead to a profound sense of dislocation, a feeling of not belonging to the story of one's lineage.

The myths families create to justify or mask their secrets are often rooted in a desire to protect. Yet, this protection comes at a cost. The myth of the perfect family, the untarnished legacy, or the infallible parent can place an immense burden on the shoulders of those who know, deep down, that the reality is far more complex. The pressure to maintain the facade can lead to a pervasive sense of isolation as individuals struggle with the dichotomy of public image and private truth.

Moreover, the energy expended in maintaining these myths can detract from the family's ability to form genuine connections. Relationships may become transactional, based on the currency of shared delusion rather than authentic emotional exchange. The fear of what might happen if the truth were to emerge can lead to a fortress mentality, where the family unit becomes insular, and outsiders are viewed with suspicion.

The consequences of these dynamics are not confined to the emotional realm. The stress of living with secrets and lies can manifest in physical ailments, a phenomenon increasingly recognized by research into psychosomatic medicine. The body keeps its ledger of the heart's unspoken burdens.

As we consider the role of secrets, lies, and family myths in the context of inherited family trauma, it becomes clear that the path to healing is paved with truth. Unraveling the tapestries of deception requires courage and a willingness to face the discomfort of revelation. Yet, through this process of uncovering and understanding the hidden narratives of our past, we can begin to free ourselves from their grip. In the light of truth, the chains of inherited trauma may begin to loosen, allowing future generations to write their own stories unencumbered by the weight of unspoken history.

The Impact of Loss and Grief

In the labyrinth of family dynamics, the echoes of loss and grief are perhaps the most profound and enduring. They are the silent currents that shape the emotional landscape of generations, carving deep channels into the collective memory of a lineage. The way a family navigates the treacherous waters of grief can leave indelible marks on its members, marks that may be passed down as inherited trauma.

When a family experiences a loss, the immediate reaction is often an outpouring of grief. This is the visible part of the iceberg, which can be acknowledged, shared, and, to some extent, socially sanctioned. However, beneath the surface lies a complex web of emotions and responses that may not find expression in tears or words. It is in this submerged silence that the seeds of inherited trauma can take root.

The bereavement process is not a linear journey with a clear endpoint. It is a cyclical and often unpredictable passage through various stages of denial, anger, bargaining, depression, and acceptance, as famously outlined by Elisabeth Kübler-Ross. Yet, not every individual or family moves through these stages in a textbook fashion. Some may become trapped in one stage, unable to advance toward healing. Others may oscillate between stages or even experience them simultaneously. This can create a family environment where grief is a constant, albeit sometimes unspoken, presence.

The impact of unresolved grief is particularly potent. When the pain of loss is not processed, it can become a silent specter at the family table, influencing interactions, decisions, and even the family's narrative about itself. Children, even those born after the loss, can inherit this unresolved grief, internalizing the sorrow and confusion they sense in their elders. They may grow up feeling something amiss, a vague melancholy they cannot quite name or understand.

Moreover, the way a family communicates about loss—or fails to communicate—can significantly shape the grief experience. In families where open expression of emotions is discouraged or where grief is considered a private matter, children may learn to suppress their feelings. This emotional stoicism can be mistaken for resilience. Still, it may be a form of avoidance that hampers grief processing. The unspoken rule that 'we do not talk about our pain' can lead to a legacy of emotional isolation and difficulty in forming deep, authentic connections.

Conversely, in families where grief is expressed excessively or dysfunctionally, children may learn to equate love with suffering. They might believe that to be a part of the family, one must carry a portion of the collective pain. This can lead to a pattern of martyrdom or co-dependency, where individuals sacrifice their well-being in the service of the family's unresolved grief.

The rituals and traditions a family adopts in the wake of loss can also play a role in the transmission of trauma. Some families may create meaningful ceremonies that honor the deceased and provide a sense of closure. Others may cling to rituals that, while intended to keep the memory of the loved one alive, inadvertently anchor the family to the moment of loss, preventing them from moving forward.

It is essential to recognize that inherited family trauma is not a destiny set in stone. With awareness and support, families can interrupt the cycle of transmitted grief. This may involve seeking therapy, fostering open communication, and creating new narratives that acknowledge the past while embracing the future. Healing inherited trauma is akin to tending to a garden that has been neglected; it requires patience, care, and the willingness to confront the weeds that choke growth. As families learn to process their grief, they can cultivate resilience and hope, ensuring that the ties that bind them are woven with love and understanding, rather than sorrow and regret.

Chapter Summary

- Family roles and expectations can be limiting and contribute to intergenerational trauma.
- Roles like the 'responsible eldest' or 'protected youngest' can stifle individual growth and perpetuate family patterns.
- Expectations may be explicit or implicit, often stemming from collective family experiences and traumas.
- These roles and expectations can trap family members in cycles of trauma and unfulfillment.
- Recognizing and challenging these roles can lead to healing and creating new, supportive family dynamics.

- Family enrichment can lead to diffused boundaries and shared trauma, while differentiation allows for individuality within family connections.
- Scapegoating within families assigns one member to bear the dysfunction, leading to isolation and potential insight for change.
- Family secrets and myths can create dysfunction and inherited trauma, with healing coming from uncovering and confronting these hidden narratives.

6

SOCIETAL REFLECTIONS: THE CULTURAL CONTEXT

Cultural Trauma and Collective Memory

Within the fabric of human life, the threads of cultural trauma and collective memory are inextricably woven together, creating patterns that tell the stories of communities and nations. These patterns, rich with the hues of shared pain and resilience, do not fade with generations; instead, they are inherited, subtly influencing the fabric of family life and individual identity.

Cultural trauma refers to a profound disruption that affects a collective. It is a wound inflicted upon the social consciousness of a community, reverberating through generations in the form of shared memories, behaviors, and values. This trauma can arise from events such as war, genocide, colonization, or natural disasters. The repercussions are not limited to those who directly experienced the event; they ripple outward, affecting those who inherit the legacy of the past.

Collective memory is the shared pool of knowledge and information in a community that extends beyond individual experiences. It encompasses the narratives that a culture preserves and passes down, shaping the identity and consciousness of its members. These memories are not static but actively maintained, constructed, and reconstructed through cultural practices such as storytelling, rituals, and education.

The interplay between cultural trauma and collective memory is complex. On the one hand, collective memory serves as a repository for the communal understanding of trauma, ensuring that the experiences of the past are not forgotten. On the other hand, it can also act as a framework through which current experiences are interpreted, potentially perpetuating the cycle of trauma.

Inherited family trauma, then, is the personal echo of these more significant cultural phenomena. It is how these historical and collective experiences shape the psychological and emotional landscape of individuals within a family. The way a family discusses (or remains silent about) past hardships, the emotional climate surrounding these narratives, and the behaviors and coping mechanisms developed in response all stem from the broader cultural context of trauma and memory.

Families may carry the weight of cultural trauma in their collective psyche, often without a conscious understanding of its origins. The stories of ancestors who survived or succumbed to great adversities are not merely tales of the past; they are the undercurrents that can influence family dynamics, parenting styles, and individual mental health. The traumas their forebears endured can shape how parents express affection, handle conflict, and deal with stress. In turn, these patterns can be passed down to their children.

The recognition of these inherited patterns is crucial for healing and growth. It allows individuals and families to contextualize their experiences within their culture's larger narrative, understand that their personal struggles may be part of a collective struggle, and find solidarity and support within their community. It also opens the door to breaking cycles of trauma by fostering awareness, empathy, and the development of new, healthier behavior patterns.

As we delve deeper into the influence of social norms and values on inherited family trauma, it becomes clear that the cultural context is both a source of wounds and a potential pathway to healing. The values a society upholds, the norms it enforces, and how it addresses—or fails to address—its collective traumas all play a role in shaping the experiences of individuals and families. Understanding this intricate relationship is essential for anyone seeking to comprehend the full scope of inherited family trauma and to contribute to the collective journey toward healing and resilience.

The Influence of Social Norms and Values

Within the complex weave of human society, the warp and weft of social norms and values shape the fabric of our daily interactions and influence how inherited family trauma is perceived, processed, and perpetuated. As we delve deeper into the cultural context of such trauma, it becomes increasingly evident that the collective ethos of a community can either exacerbate the silent suffering passed down through generations or provide a nurturing ground for healing and transformation.

Social norms, the unwritten rules that govern behavior in groups and societies, often dictate the response to trauma. In some cultures, stoicism and resilience are highly valued, and individuals are expected to bear their burdens silently without outwardly acknowledging their pain. This cultural expectation can lead to a suppression of traumatic experiences, as individuals may feel compelled to maintain a facade of strength and normalcy. The internalization of trauma, in this context, becomes a hidden legacy, one that is silently inherited by offspring who may sense the unspoken anguish of their forebears but lack the vocabulary or permission to address it.

Conversely, open communication and emotional expression can foster an environment where discussing past hurts is not only allowed but encouraged. In such societies, the acknowledgment of trauma is seen as a step towards healing, and sharing one's story is viewed as an act of courage rather than a sign of weakness. This cultural milieu can mitigate the transmission of trauma by creating spaces for dialogue, reflection, and collective support.

The influence of social norms and values extends to the institutions that uphold them. Educational systems, religious organizations, and the media all play pivotal roles in either reinforcing the silence surrounding inherited trauma or challenging the status quo. Educational curricula that study historical traumas and their impact on present generations can enlighten young minds about the complexities of inherited pain. Religious and spiritual practices that offer rituals for mourning and forgiveness can provide solace and a path to release the burdens of the past. Meanwhile, media representation that humanizes the experiences of those carrying the weight of ancestral trauma can shift public perception and foster empathy.

However, this cultural scaffolding has its challenges. Norms and values are not static; they evolve with time and can be subject to the whims of those in power. What is considered taboo today may be openly discussed tomorrow, and vice versa. This fluidity can leave individuals grappling with inherited trauma in a liminal space, uncertain of whether their experiences will be met with understanding or judgment.

Moreover, the intersectionality of identity—race, gender, class, and more—complicates the landscape of inherited trauma. Marginalized groups may face additional barriers in seeking recognition and healing for their inherited wounds, as societal prejudices can silence their narratives or minimize their pain. The interplay of these identities with cultural norms and values can either compound the trauma or catalyze a collective movement toward healing.

As we consider the influence of social norms and values on inherited family trauma, it is crucial to recognize the power of cultural change. By challenging harmful norms and advocating for values that promote healing and understanding, societies can begin to address the deep-seated traumas passed down through generations. Through this cultural evolution, we can hope to see a future where the legacy of trauma is not one of silent suffering but of resilience and renewal.

Immigration, Displacement, and Diaspora

Within the mosaic of human existence, the threads of immigration, displacement, and diaspora are interwoven with complex patterns of inherited family trauma. These phenomena, often driven by necessity, ambition, or survival, carry the weight of cultural upheaval and the silent echoes of ancestral struggles. As families traverse borders and oceans, they do not merely transport belongings; they carry the intangible legacy of their forebears, a legacy that often includes the trauma of leaving behind everything familiar.

The act of immigration is a disruption of the narrative continuity of a family's history. This decision can be both empowering and disorienting, as it promises new beginnings while severing ties with the past. The immigrant journey is fraught with challenges, from the physical dangers of the journey to the psychological toll of adjusting to a new society. The displacement accompanying immigration can lead to a sense of rootlessness, a feeling of being suspended between two worlds, neither entirely belonging to the old nor entirely accepted by the new.

For children of immigrants, this sense of displacement is inherited, often without the accompanying memories of the homeland. They are born into a diaspora, a scattered community whose shared history is marked by the collective trauma of dislocation. These children may grapple with a fragmented identity, piecing together their sense of self from stories, traditions, and the lingering effects of their parent's experiences. The trauma of immigration does not dissipate with the crossing of a border; it lingers, manifesting in the emotional and cultural dissonance that can permeate a family for generations.

The cultural context of the new society plays a pivotal role in shaping the immigrant experience. Acceptance, integration, and the opportunity to thrive are not guaranteed. Instead, immigrants often encounter barriers that hinder their ability to participate fully in their new home's social fabric. Language barriers, economic disparities, and cultural misunderstandings can exacerbate the sense of otherness, reinforcing the trauma of displacement.

Moreover, the diaspora community can serve as both a sanctuary and a source of tension. Within it is a collective memory of the homeland and a shared understanding of the immigrant experience. Yet, there can also be pressure to conform to the expectations of the diaspora to maintain cultural purity in a constantly changing land. This pressure can create a rift between generations as younger members navigate the delicate balance of honoring their heritage while seeking to belong in a society that may view them with suspicion or indifference.

The inherited trauma of immigration, displacement, and diaspora is thus a complex interplay of loss, adaptation, and resilience. It is a narrative that unfolds over lifetimes, with each generation adding its chapter to the family story. As we delve deeper into the societal implications of these experiences, we must also consider how racism, discrimination, and the intergenerational impact of these prejudices further shape the lives of those who have left their homelands in search of a better future.

Racism, Discrimination, and Intergenerational Impact

Throughout our existence, the threads of racism and discrimination are woven with particular darkness, their shadows stretching across generations, imprinting a legacy of pain and resilience in the fabric of family narratives. The intergenerational impact of these societal scourges is profound, often manifesting in ways that are subtle yet deeply entrenched within the psyche of those who bear the weight of historical injustices.

The concept of inherited family trauma is not merely an abstract psychological theory; it is a palpable reality for many. The silent whisper of anxiety lingers in the hearts of parents as they prepare their children for the prejudices they may face. It is the internalized oppression that stifles ambition and the unspoken grief that accompanies the stories of ancestors who endured unimaginable hardships simply because of their race or ethnicity.

For communities that have been marginalized, the trauma does not begin and end with a single event or generation. It is perpetuated through systemic inequalities, microaggressions in daily interactions, and the collective memory of historical atrocities that are too often sanitized or erased from the dominant cultural narrative. The psychological armor developed as a defense mechanism against these assaults does not quickly shed; it becomes part of the inheritance passed down, a complex interplay of resilience and vulnerability.

This inherited trauma can manifest in various forms, from the heightened vigilance that comes with the knowledge of one's skin color being a potential threat to others to the deep-seated fear of authority figures whose roles have historically been to oppress rather than to protect. It can lead to a profound sense of dislocation, even in one's homeland, and the internalization of negative stereotypes that erode self-esteem and foster a sense of otherness.

Yet, within this landscape of pain, there is also the potential for profound strength and solidarity. Families and communities share not only the burden of their collective trauma but also the wisdom and coping strategies that have allowed them to survive and, in many cases, to thrive despite the odds. The stories of resistance and triumph are as much a part of the legacy as the stories of suffering.

Understanding the intergenerational impact of racism and discrimination is crucial in the journey towards healing. It requires an acknowledgment of the past, an awareness of the present, and a commitment to a future where such legacies no longer dictate the boundaries of one's life. It calls for a compassionate and informed approach to addressing the wounds that, though invisible to the eye, are etched deeply into the hearts and minds of those affected.

As we move towards a cultural context in which healing is possible and actively pursued, we must recognize the resilience cultivated through generations of adversity. The path to healing is not linear or uniform. Still, it is paved with the collective efforts of individuals and communities who seek to transform the pain of the past into a foundation for a more just and empathetic world.

Healing in a Cultural Context

Within the complex fabric of human existence, the threads of trauma, particularly those inherited from our forebears, are woven with a resilience that is as commendable as it is complex. As we delve into healing within a cultural context, we must recognize that the path to recovery is not merely an individual journey. Still, it is deeply embedded within the cultural fabric that clothes our collective identity.

Culture, in its vast and varied forms, provides a backdrop against which the narrative of trauma and healing unfolds. Within this cultural framework, individuals find the symbols, rituals, and collective stories that can hinder or facilitate the healing process. To understand healing in a cultural context, we must first acknowledge that the very definition of trauma and the strategies for coping with it are culturally contingent.

The cultural context offers a repository of healing practices honed over generations. These practices, from traditional ceremonies and rites to storytelling and communal gatherings, serve as a conduit for expressing and processing the pain often buried within the collective psyche. They allow for the sharing of burdens, the validation of experiences, and the re-establishment of a sense of belonging and identity that trauma can disrupt.

Moreover, the role of the community must be balanced in the healing process. In many cultures, the community acts as a mirror reflecting the individual's pain, thus acknowledging its existence and legitimizing the individual's experience. This communal recognition is the first step towards healing, as it breaks the isolation that trauma can impose. The community then becomes a source of support, offering a network of relationships that can provide practical assistance, emotional comfort, and a path back to social engagement.

However, the cultural context can also present unique challenges to healing. Cultural stigmas attached to mental health, a legacy of silence surrounding trauma, or a collective identity that may prioritize endurance over the expression of suffering can all act as barriers. In such environments, seeking help may be seen as a deviation from the norm, and those who do so may face misunderstanding or ostracization.

Navigating these cultural complexities is crucial to fostering cultural competence among those who provide support and therapy. Understanding the cultural narratives and values that shape an individual's worldview can guide the healing process in a direction that resonates with their identity and experiences. Therapists and healers must recognize and incorporate cultural strengths into their practices, whether through language, metaphor, or culturally specific therapeutic interventions.

In the broader societal context, there is a growing recognition of the need for culturally sensitive approaches to healing. This includes acknowledging historical injustices and their ongoing impact on communities and ensuring that institutional support systems are attuned to the cultural dimensions of trauma. Policies and programs designed to address inherited family trauma must be crafted with an awareness of the cultural narratives that underpin the communities they aim to serve.

Therefore, healing in a cultural context is an intricate dance between honoring the wisdom of traditional healing practices and integrating the insights of contemporary therapeutic approaches. It is about creating spaces where individuals can find their voice within the chorus of their community and where the echoes of past traumas can be transformed into narratives of resilience and hope. As we continue to explore the multifaceted nature of inherited family trauma, it is this cultural lens that allows us to see the full spectrum of the human capacity for healing and growth.

Chapter Summary

- Cultural trauma refers to a profound disruption in a community, affecting collective memory and identity across generations.
- Collective memory is the shared knowledge within a community that shapes its members' identity and is actively maintained through cultural practices.
- The interplay between cultural trauma and collective memory can perpetuate trauma cycles or serve as a repository for communal understanding.
- Inherited family trauma is how historical and collective experiences shape individuals' psychological and emotional landscapes within a family.
- The traumas endured by ancestors can influence family dynamics, parenting styles, and individual mental health.
- Recognizing inherited patterns is critical to healing, allowing individuals to contextualize their struggles within a larger collective narrative.
- Social norms and values influence how inherited family trauma is perceived and processed, either reinforcing silence or fostering healing environments.
- Immigration, displacement, and diaspora introduce complex patterns of inherited trauma, including cultural upheaval and identity fragmentation.

7

THE JOURNEY WITHIN: PERSONAL STORIES

Voices from the Shadows: Personal Narratives

In the quiet recesses of our minds, where the echoes of our ancestors' experiences still resonate, we find the personal narratives that shape our understanding of inherited family trauma. These are the voices from the shadows, the stories that often go untold yet hold the power to influence generations.

One such narrative belongs to Maria, whose grandfather survived a war that ravaged his homeland and psyche. Though he never spoke of the horrors he witnessed, the silent ripples of his pain lapped through the family lineage. Maria grew up in a household where the air was thick with unspoken grief, a grief that she could taste but not name. It was only in her thirties, when she began to unravel her anxiety and inexplicable fears that she traced their roots to the grandfather she had never met. His trauma, unaddressed and unacknowledged, had become a silent heirloom.

Then there's David, whose mother endured a tumultuous and abusive marriage. David learned to walk on eggshells, internalizing the volatility of his childhood home. As an adult, he found himself inexplicably drawn to partners who mirrored the chaos he had known as a child. It was a pattern etched into his being, a learned response to a trauma that predated his memories. It was only through recognizing this pattern that he began seeking a different path that led away from the shadows of inherited pain.

These stories, and countless others like them, reveal the intricate web of our familial tapestries. Each thread is a story, a memory, a piece of a larger picture we carry. The weight of these inherited narratives can be heavy, and the journey to understanding and healing is often solitary. Yet, it is within the sharing of these personal narratives that we find a collective solace. When we give voice to the shadows, we illuminate the paths that our ancestors could not find, and in doing so, we forge new trails for ourselves and the generations to come.

Storytelling is not merely a recounting of events but an act of liberation. We acknowledge the depth of our shared human experience by bringing these personal narratives into the light. We validate not only our pain but also the pain of those who came before us. This acknowledgment is the first step toward healing, a step that many find themselves taking within the pages of their own lives long before they ever seek the guidance of therapists or the solace of support groups.

As we turn the page from the voices that have long been relegated to the shadows, we prepare to explore the transformative power of acknowledgment and validation. It is here that we will delve into the profound impact that recognition and acceptance can have on the journey toward healing inherited family trauma.

The Power of Acknowledgment and Validation

In the weave of human existence, the threads of our ancestors' hardships are often interwoven with our own, creating patterns that can either confine or guide us. As we delve into the personal stories of those who carry inherited family trauma, we uncover a profound truth: the act of acknowledging and validating these inherited pains is not merely a step toward healing—it is a transformative power in its own right.

For many, the journey within begins with a whisper—a sense that the emotions and reactions they experience are not solely their own. It's a realization that the anxiety felt before a family gathering or the inexplicable sadness that clouds a seemingly happy occasion may echo past generations' unresolved grief and suffering. These whispers grow louder, demanding attention, and the courageous act of listening takes the first steps toward acknowledgment.

Acknowledgment is a declaration that the trauma endured by previous generations matters. It is a conscious effort to shine a light on the dark corners of a family's history, to say, "This happened, and it affected us." It validates the pain that has silently shaped lives and relationships. In acknowledging inherited trauma, individuals permit themselves to explore the depth of their emotional inheritance without judgment or dismissal.

Validation follows acknowledgment like a balm. It is the empathetic response that says, "Your feelings are real, and they are worthy of attention." It is the external confirmation from loved ones, therapists, or support groups that the struggle one faces is legitimate and understood. Validation provides a mirror in which the true impact of inherited trauma is reflected, allowing those affected to see themselves and their experiences clearly, perhaps for the first time.

The power of acknowledgment and validation lies in their ability to break the cycle of silence that often surrounds inherited trauma. They create a space where stories can be shared without fear of stigma or disbelief. In this space, individuals find that their narratives are not isolated incidents but part of a more extensive, communal history. This realization fosters a sense of belonging and connection, vital for healing.

Moreover, acknowledgment and validation are not passive acts but dynamic processes that engage the intellect and emotions. They require an ongoing commitment to self-awareness and compassion for oneself and the generations that came before. Through these processes, individuals differentiate which parts of their emotional landscape are genuinely theirs and which are inherited. This differentiation is crucial for developing a sense of autonomy and making conscious choices about which legacies to carry forward and which to release.

As we journey with those who have embarked on this path of acknowledgment and validation, we witness the emergence of resilience and strength. Facing inherited trauma with honesty and compassion becomes a powerful testament to the human spirit's capacity for growth and transformation. It is a reminder that while we may inherit the traumas of our forebears, we also inherit their courage and ability to overcome.

In the next breaths of our exploration, we will gaze toward the turning points and catalysts that propel individuals from acknowledgment to action, from understanding to change. These moments mark the beginning of a new legacy that honors the past while forging a healthier, more conscious future.

Turning Points and Catalysts for Change

In life, each thread represents a story, a lineage, and a history passed down through generations. The colors may fade or change, but the fabric remains connected, often carrying the subtle yet profound imprints of inherited family trauma. As we delve into the personal narratives that make up the journey within, we encounter individuals at the precipice of transformation—moments that serve as turning points and catalysts for change.

These stories are not mere anecdotes; they are the living, breathing experiences of people who have faced the daunting task of confronting the silent legacies that have shaped their existence. The turning points are as diverse as the individuals themselves. Yet, they share a common thread: the realization that the cycles of the past need not dictate the patterns of the future.

For some, the catalyst for change is a singular, life-altering event—a birth, a death, a confrontation with mortality that brings the hidden traumas of the past to the surface. For others, it is a slow awakening, a series of subtle cues that accumulate over time, leading to the undeniable truth that their pain is not entirely their own.

One such story is that of Elena, a third-generation immigrant whose grandparents fled war-torn Europe. The resilience they needed to rebuild their lives in a new country was a source of pride in her family. Yet, beneath the surface of that resilience was an undercurrent of unspoken anxiety and hyper-vigilance that permeated Elena's upbringing. It wasn't until Elena faced her battle with anxiety that she began to unravel the threads of inherited trauma, recognizing the patterns that had been invisibly woven into her behavior.

Another narrative unfolds with Michael, whose father's unexplained outbursts of anger and subsequent withdrawal into silence were the backdrop of his childhood. It was only upon becoming a father himself that Michael felt the weight of unprocessed grief—grief that he later discovered was rooted in his father's experience as a child of an alcoholic parent. The birth of his daughter was the turning point. This catalyst propelled him to seek help and break the cycle of emotional suppression that had been handed down to him.

While deeply personal, these turning points are also universal in their resonance. They are the moments when the past is held up to the light, examined, and understood not as a determinant of fate but as a map that has guided one to the present. With this understanding comes the possibility of charting a new course that honors the journey of those who came before while forging a path toward healing.

The courage to confront inherited family trauma is not a solitary endeavor. It is a collective journey that requires empathy, support, and the shared wisdom of those who have walked similar paths. As we witness these stories of transformation, we are reminded that the legacy of the past need not be a burden. Instead, it can be the catalyst that inspires us to heal, grow, and redefine the narrative for future generations.

In this journey within, the turning points and catalysts for change are not just markers of individual growth; they are beacons of hope for all who seek to understand the intricate web of inherited trauma. They are a testament to the human spirit's capacity to transcend the confines of history and embrace the potential for renewal.

Legacy Bearers: The Weight of History

Within our human experience, the threads of our ancestors' hardships are often interwoven with our own, creating patterns that may go unnoticed until we take a closer look. As we delve into the personal stories of those who carry the weight of history, we find that the legacy of inherited family trauma is not just a relic of the past but a living, breathing presence in the lives of descendants.

Consider Sarah, whose grandfather survived a brutal war. The horrors he witnessed were etched into the silence that filled their home. Sarah grew up in the shadow of unspoken grief, a quiet understanding that some things were too painful to voice. It was only when she found herself grappling with inexplicable anxiety that the connection to her grandfather's unhealed wounds became clear. Her journey to address her struggles led her to uncover the buried stories of her family's past, revealing the unseen influence of inherited trauma.

Then there's Adam, whose family history was riddled with addiction. The cycle seemed unbreakable, each generation succumbing to the same destructive patterns. It was as if the addiction was part of the family legacy, passed down like a dark heirloom. But Adam's story took a different turn. Through introspection and therapy, he began to unravel the emotional legacy that fueled these patterns. His commitment to healing became a beacon of hope, illuminating a path forward for himself and future generations.

These narratives are not isolated instances but echoes of a collective human experience. The weight of history is carried in the hearts and minds of those who come after, often manifesting in subtle yet profound ways. It is a weight that can bend the branches of a family tree. Yet, it also has the potential to foster a deep sense of resilience and understanding.

As we explore these personal stories, we see that the journey within is not a solitary one. It is a shared expedition, a quest that connects us to the generations that came before and those that will follow. The legacy of trauma, while heavy, also presents an opportunity for growth and transformation. Through the acknowledgment and processing of this pain, healing can begin for the individual and the lineage as a whole.

Inherited family trauma is not a sentence to be served but a challenge to be met with compassion and courage. As we witness these stories, we are reminded of the strength in vulnerability and the power of confronting our inherited shadows. The journey within is a passage through time, a chance to mend the fractures of the past and forge a future where the weight of history is acknowledged, respected, and, ultimately, transcended.

The Quest for Identity and Belonging

In the tapestry of human experience, the threads of our ancestors' lives are interwoven with our own, often in ways we are only beginning to understand. The journey to comprehend our identity and the sense of belonging we yearn for is not merely a path we tread in isolation. It is a quest that spans generations, a search for self that reaches back into the depths of family history, where the echoes of inherited trauma reside.

The stories we carry within us are not always our own. They are endowed to us by those who came before, often passed down silently through the subtlest of behaviors, the quietest of fears, and the most unspoken of expectations. These inherited narratives shape our sense of self, our view of the world, and our place within it. They can bind us to a legacy of resilience and strength or shackle us to cycles of pain and loss that we struggle to understand, let alone break free from.

Consider Madeleine, whose grandfather survived a brutal war. He returned home a changed man, his spirit burdened with memories too painful to share. His silence was a fortress that not even his children could penetrate. Madeleine grew up in the shadow of this unspoken history, feeling the weight of an invisible inheritance. It was only when she began to explore her family's past that she realized her battles with anxiety were not solely her own but also silent whispers of her grandfather's unhealed wounds.

Then there's John, whose mother endured a tumultuous and abusive relationship. The trauma she experienced was an uninvited guest in their home, one that lingered long after the relationship ended. John learned to walk on eggshells, internalizing a sense of instability that would manifest in his relationships. It was a pattern he recognized only after embarking on a journey of self-discovery, one that led him to confront the pain his mother had inadvertently handed down to him.

These personal stories, and countless others like them, reveal the complex interplay between our quest for identity and the inherited traumas that shape our lives. They underscore the importance of understanding our family history, not to assign blame or to dwell in the past, but to gain insight into the origins of our deepest struggles. This understanding can be a powerful catalyst for healing, breaking the cycles that have held us captive, and reclaiming our life narratives.

As we delve into the layers of our family's past, we often find that our search for identity is intertwined with a need for belonging. To belong is to connect, to find our place within the continuum of our lineage, and to recognize the resilience that has carried our family through adversity. It is also to acknowledge the pain and offer compassion to those who came before us and ourselves as we grapple with the legacies we carry.

In embracing the full spectrum of our family's narrative, we can begin to forge a new sense of identity that honors our history without being confined by it. We can build a sense of belonging that is rooted not in past traumas but in the understanding and healing that the present allows. This is the essence of our quest, a deeply personal journey and inextricably linked to the generations that have paved the way for our own steps.

As we continue to navigate the intricate paths of our inner worlds, let us do so with the knowledge that our search for identity and belonging is a profound act of healing, one that has the power to transform not only our own lives but the legacy we leave for those who will follow.

Chapter Summary

- The chapter discusses the impact of inherited family trauma on individuals through personal narratives.
- Maria's story illustrates how unspoken grief from her grandfather's war experiences affected her own life.
- David's narrative shows how the chaos of his mother's abusive marriage influenced his adult relationships.
- Acknowledgment and validation of inherited trauma are presented as crucial steps toward healing.
- The chapter emphasizes the transformative power of recognizing and accepting the pain of past generations.
- Turning points and catalysts for change are highlighted as pivotal in breaking the cycle of inherited trauma.
- The weight of history and the responsibility of legacy bearers to confront and heal from past traumas are explored.
- The quest for identity and belonging is tied to understanding and healing from family history and inherited trauma.

8

PATHWAYS TO HEALING: THERAPEUTIC APPROACHES

Traditional Psychotherapy and Family Trauma

In the realm of traditional psychotherapy, the exploration and treatment of inherited family trauma necessitates a nuanced understanding of the human psyche and the intricate web of familial relationships. It is within this context that therapists often turn to time-honored approaches such as psychodynamic therapy, family systems therapy, and cognitive-behavioral therapy (CBT) to unravel the complex layers of intergenerational trauma.

Psychodynamic therapy delves into the unconscious mind, seeking to uncover the deep-seated roots of emotional suffering that may span multiple generations. It operates on the premise that the unresolved issues of our ancestors can insidiously influence our emotional landscape. Through the therapeutic alliance, individuals are encouraged to explore their family history, identifying patterns and unconscious scripts that have been passed down. This introspective journey can be both profound and challenging, as it often involves confronting painful memories and long-standing defense mechanisms.

On the other hand, family systems therapy adopts a more holistic view, considering the family as an interconnected unit where each member's behavior affects the whole. It posits that trauma is not just an individual experience but one that permeates the family system, creating ripples that can affect multiple generations. Engaging multiple family members in the therapeutic process aims to foster understanding and healing within the relational dynamics. It is through the reconfiguration of these dynamics and the establishment of healthier communication patterns that families can begin to break the cycle of trauma.

CBT, with its structured approach, offers another avenue for addressing the cognitive distortions that may arise from inherited trauma. It helps individuals recognize and challenge maladaptive thought patterns, equipping them with coping strategies and ultimately transforming their emotional responses. While CBT is often more focused on present-day symptoms and behaviors, it can still be adapted to address the historical context of these issues, providing a bridge between past traumas and current experiences.

Each of these therapeutic modalities offers unique insights and tools for healing. Yet, they share a common goal: to help individuals and families understand the origins of their pain, develop resilience, and cultivate a sense of agency over their lives. The therapeutic journey is one of reclamation as clients learn to reclaim their narratives from the shadows of the past.

As we transition from the traditional psychotherapy methods to the innovative therapies in the following section, it is essential to recognize that each approach serves as a stepping stone toward healing. The following therapies we will explore, such as Eye Movement Desensitization and Reprocessing (EMDR) and Somatic Experiencing, build upon the foundation laid by traditional methods, offering new perspectives and techniques for individuals grappling with the echoes of family trauma. While distinct in their methodologies, these modalities continue the overarching mission of traditional therapy: to facilitate a journey of healing that honors both the individual and the collective story of the family.

Innovative Therapies: EMDR, Somatic Experiencing, and More

As we delve deeper into the therapeutic approaches for inherited family trauma, it is essential to recognize the value of innovative therapies that have emerged in recent years. These modalities, while not as traditional as the psychotherapy discussed earlier, offer unique pathways to healing that may resonate with individuals for whom conventional treatments have been less effective.

Eye Movement Desensitization and Reprocessing (EMDR) is one such therapy that has garnered attention for its effectiveness in treating trauma. Developed by Francine Shapiro in the late 1980s, EMDR is predicated on the idea that the mind can heal from psychological trauma much as the body recovers from physical trauma. When a disturbing event occurs, it can get locked in the nervous system with the original pictures, sounds, thoughts, feelings, and body sensations. EMDR unlocks the nervous system and allows the mind and body to process the experience. This is particularly relevant for inherited family trauma, as it may help individuals process and integrate traumatic memories that are not directly on their own but have been passed down through generations.

EMDR involves the therapist guiding the client through a series of lateral eye movements while recalling the traumatic event, which is believed to work by mimicking the psychological state we enter during REM sleep. This state may facilitate the integration of complex memories and emotions. For those grappling with inherited family trauma, EMDR offers a way to address the complex layers of intergenerational pain without the necessity of a linear narrative, which can sometimes be elusive.

Another approach that has shown promise is somatic observing (SE), developed by Dr. Peter Levine. SE is grounded in the understanding that trauma may manifest as physical symptoms in the body. It focuses on the client's perceived body sensations (or somatic experiences) rather than solely on the cognitive or emotional aspects of trauma. By paying close attention to the body's responses, individuals learn to release and resolve the physical tension in the aftermath of traumatic events. This method can be particularly beneficial for inherited family trauma, as it addresses the often unconscious and somatically stored trauma responses that are passed down from one generation to the next.

SE therapy is a gentle and gradual process, allowing individuals to develop increased tolerance to complex bodily sensations and suppressed emotions. It is a holistic approach that not only acknowledges the psychological impact of trauma but also the bodily and instinctual dimensions of our experience. This can be a powerful method for those who carry the weight of their ancestors' traumas in their bodies, perhaps in ways they cannot fully articulate through words alone.

Beyond EMDR and SE, other innovative therapies have been developed to address trauma, such as Internal Family Systems (IFS) and Narrative Therapy. These approaches offer different lenses to view and heal from inherited family trauma, emphasizing the diversity of our inner experiences and the power of re-authoring our stories.

As we continue to explore the spectrum of therapeutic options available, it becomes clear that the journey to healing from inherited family trauma is not a one-size-fits-all endeavor. It is a deeply personal process that may require a combination of approaches, and individuals must find the path that resonates most profoundly with their unique experiences and needs. The following steps in this journey involve turning inward as we consider the role of mindfulness and meditation in fostering an environment within ourselves that is conducive to healing and growth.

The Role of Mindfulness and Meditation

In the journey toward healing inherited family trauma, we find ourselves at the crossroads of ancient wisdom and modern psychological understanding. Mindfulness and meditation, steeped in historical reverence, have emerged as powerful tools in the therapeutic landscape. Their role in addressing the wounds of the past is not merely supportive; it is transformative.

Mindfulness, the art of being fully present and engaged with the here and now without judgment, offers a profound gateway to self-awareness. For individuals grappling with the echoes of familial suffering, mindfulness provides a means to observe their internal landscape without being overwhelmed by the intensity of emotions and memories that may arise. It is a practice of cultivating a compassionate witness within oneself, a witness that acknowledges pain without becoming entangled in it.

Meditation, a companion to mindfulness, invites a deeper exploration into the self. Through various forms, from focused attention to movement-based practices, meditation allows individuals to step back from the constant chatter of the mind and the often unconscious narratives inherited from family history. In the stillness that meditation fosters, there is space for new insights to emerge—insights that can lead to the unraveling of generational patterns.

The therapeutic power of these practices lies in their ability to alter the relationship one has with one's thoughts and feelings. Research has shed light on how mindfulness and meditation can change the brain's structure and function, leading to increased emotional regulation, decreased reactivity to stress, and improved mental clarity. These neurological shifts are particularly beneficial for those whose inherited trauma has left them with a heightened stress response or a pervasive sense of anxiety.

Moreover, mindfulness and meditation do not require one to relive the traumatic events of the past, which can be retraumatizing for some. Instead, these practices encourage a gentle and gradual healing process that honors the individual's pace and capacity for growth. They empower individuals to reclaim their agency, often diminished by the weight of trauma, by offering them the skills to manage their emotional states and to make conscious choices in their thoughts and actions.

In the therapeutic setting, mindfulness and meditation can seamlessly integrate into client work. Therapists may guide individuals through mindfulness exercises during sessions, teaching them how to ground themselves in the present moment when distressing memories surface. Meditation can also be introduced as a daily practice that supports the therapeutic process by providing a consistent framework for self-reflection and emotional balance.

As we move forward in our exploration of healing modalities, it is essential to recognize the collective dimension of inherited family trauma. The following section will delve into the significance of group work and community healing, where the shared experience of trauma and recovery fosters a sense of solidarity and collective transformation. Mindfulness and meditation, while often practiced individually, can also be adapted to these communal settings, offering a shared language for understanding and healing.

Group Work and Community Healing

On the path to recovery from generational family trauma, the solitary pursuit of mindfulness and meditation can be significantly enriched by the embrace of collective experiences. Group work and community healing offer a powerful antidote to the isolation that often accompanies the deep-seated wounds of intergenerational pain. Within the safe confines of a group, individuals find solace and the shared strength to confront and reframe the narratives that have been passed down through their lineage.

The efficacy of group therapy lies in its capacity to mirror the familial and social dynamics that may have contributed to the perpetuation of trauma. Within this microcosm, individuals can explore the impact of their inherited stories, behaviors, and emotions in a space that fosters empathy and understanding. The group setting provides a platform for multiple voices, allowing participants to witness and participate in each other's healing processes, which can be profoundly validating and transformative.

One of the critical components of group work is the sense of belonging it instills. For many, realizing they are not alone in their struggles is revelatory and liberating. The shared experiences within the group can dismantle the walls of loneliness and secrecy that often surround family trauma. As members articulate their experiences and listen to others, they recognize familiar patterns and themes, which can lead to a collective sense of identity and purpose.

The role of the facilitator in this setting is to guide the process with sensitivity and expertise, ensuring that the environment remains respectful and supportive. Skilled facilitators encourage expressing emotions and exchanging perspectives while maintaining boundaries that protect the group's integrity. They help members navigate the delicate balance between personal introspection and communal interaction, fostering a space where healing can occur individually and collectively.

Community healing extends the principles of group work to a broader context, recognizing that the roots of trauma often lie in historical, cultural, or societal events. Engaging with one's community can provide a larger framework for understanding the origins of family trauma and how it has been sustained over generations. Community-based initiatives include public storytelling events, healing circles, or cultural rituals, which can validate individual experiences and promote collective catharsis.

In these communal spaces, the shared acknowledgment of past injustices and the commitment to breaking cycles of pain can be a potent force for change. Here, individuals can find a sense of agency, learning to advocate for their own healing and the transformation of the community as a whole. The collective endeavor to heal can lead to new traditions and practices that honor the past while actively shaping a more conscious and compassionate future.

As we delve deeper into the therapeutic approaches to inherited family trauma, it becomes clear that the integration of group work and community healing is not just beneficial but essential. The collective journey mirrors our own experiences and offers a window into the shared human condition, reminding us that our stories are interconnected and that our healing, too, is a shared responsibility.

Integrating New Narratives

In the journey toward healing from inherited family trauma, we have explored the power of collective experiences through group work and the solidarity found within community healing. As we transition from the shared to the personal, we delve into individual narratives and the profound impact of integrating new, empowering stories into one's life.

The human psyche is akin to a tapestry woven with the threads of our experiences, beliefs, and the stories we tell ourselves about who we are and where we come from. For those carrying the weight of inherited trauma, the narrative often includes themes of pain, loss, and a sense of certainty that the past seals one's fate. However, integrating new narratives offers hope, illuminating the path to rewriting one's story with autonomy and resilience.

The therapeutic approach to integrating new narratives begins with acknowledging the existing story. It requires a compassionate and empathetic exploration of the trauma narrative passed down through generations. This understanding is not to dwell on the suffering but to recognize its influence on the individual's life script. By bringing these stories into the light, we can see them not as unchangeable truths but as narratives that have been shaped by many hands and can be reshaped by the one holding the pen now.

The next step is the deliberate and often challenging work of crafting a new narrative. This is not about denying or erasing the past but expanding the story to include the strength, survival, and lessons learned from ancestors' experiences. It is about recognizing that while the trauma is a part of history, it does not have to dictate the future. Individuals are encouraged to identify and amplify their values, aspirations, and dreams, weaving these into the fabric of their new narrative.

Therapists may use various techniques to facilitate this process, such as narrative therapy, which involves re-authoring one's story, or cognitive-behavioral approaches that help to reframe and challenge unhelpful beliefs. Creative expression also serves as a powerful tool, allowing for the externalization of the trauma narrative and the active construction of a new one through art, writing, or drama.

As individuals begin to integrate these new narratives, they often experience a shift in their identity. They start to see themselves not as victims of their family's past but as active agents in their own lives. This redefined self-concept opens up possibilities for healing within themselves, their relationships, and the broader family system. The new narrative becomes a legacy of its own, one that can be passed down to future generations, marked not by the scars of trauma but by the resilience and conscious creation of a hopeful future.

Integrating new narratives is a profound act of reclamation and transformation. It is a testament to the human capacity for change and the power of stories to shape our reality. As we continue to explore the pathways to healing, we recognize that each individual's journey is unique. Yet, there is a universal thread that connects us all—the enduring ability to rewrite our stories and, in doing so, to reclaim our lives.

Chapter Summary

- Traditional psychotherapy approaches like psychodynamic therapy, family systems therapy, and CBT are used to address inherited family trauma.
- Psychodynamic therapy explores the unconscious mind to uncover emotional suffering that may span generations.

- Family systems therapy views the family as an interconnected unit and addresses trauma as a shared experience within this system.
- CBT focuses on present-day symptoms and behaviors, helping individuals recognize and challenge maladaptive thought patterns.
- Innovative therapies like EMDR and Somatic Experiencing offer new techniques for dealing with intergenerational trauma.
- EMDR facilitates the processing of traumatic memories through eye movements, while SE focuses on resolving physical tension related to trauma.
- Mindfulness and meditation are transformative practices that help individuals manage their emotional states and foster self-awareness.
- Group work and community healing provide a collective space for individuals to share their experiences and find solidarity in their journey toward healing.

9

THE RIPPLE EFFECT: RELATIONSHIPS AND SOCIETY

Interpersonal Relationships and Trauma Patterns

Within relationships, the threads of inherited family trauma are often woven so subtly into the fabric of our interactions that they can go unnoticed, yet their influence is profound. These inherited patterns of behavior and emotional responses passed down from one generation to the next can shape the dynamics of our closest relationships in complex and far-reaching ways.

The concept of inherited family trauma suggests that the unresolved traumas of our ancestors do not simply vanish with time. Instead, they linger, silently scripting the emotional landscapes of those who follow. This can manifest in a myriad of ways within interpersonal relationships. For instance, a parent who experienced abandonment as a child may, despite their best intentions, struggle with attachment issues, inadvertently creating a sense of insecurity in their children. Similarly, a partner who has inherited a legacy of mistrust may find it challenging to cultivate a healthy, trusting relationship with their spouse.

These patterns are not merely psychological but can be deeply embedded in the nonverbal cues and emotional responses integral to human connection. The way one might flinch at a raised voice or the difficulty another might have in expressing affection can be echoes of past traumas that were never fully processed or understood by the individuals who first experienced them. It is through these unspoken languages that the legacy of trauma is often most powerfully transmitted.

The impact of such inherited trauma on relationships can be profound. It can lead to cycles of dysfunction, where individuals unwittingly recreate the emotional environments that were modeled to them in childhood. This can result in a cascade of relational challenges, including communication breakdowns, emotional volatility, and a pervasive sense of disconnection. Even more insidiously, these patterns can become normalized within families, creating a blueprint for relationships that is difficult to recognize as harmful because it is so familiar.

However, it is essential to approach this subject not with resignation but with a sense of empowered awareness. Recognizing these patterns is the first step in breaking the cycle. It allows individuals to understand that their struggles within relationships may not be solely of their own making but rather part of a larger historical context. This understanding can foster empathy for oneself and family members grappling with the legacy of past traumas.

By bringing these patterns into the light, individuals and families can begin the work of healing. This often involves developing a new emotional vocabulary that includes the language of validation, understanding, and resilience. It may also require the support of therapeutic interventions that specifically address the complexities of inherited trauma, helping individuals to disentangle their emotional responses from those of their ancestors.

As we delve deeper into the understanding of how inherited family trauma shapes our relationships, we pave the way for more conscious and intentional interactions. This journey of awareness and healing is about looking back and moving forward with a new sense of clarity and purpose. It is about rewriting the emotional scripts handed down to us and choosing to foster relationships rooted in health, understanding, and compassion.

In this pursuit of transformation, the role of community cannot be understated. It is within the collective embrace of a trauma-informed society that individuals find the strength and support to heal not only themselves but also the relational fabric that binds us all. As we transition to exploring the concept of trauma-informed communities, we carry with us the understanding that healing inherited family trauma is not a solitary endeavor but a communal one, where the collective wisdom and compassion of the community play an integral role in facilitating individual and familial healing.

Trauma-Informed Communities

When discussing human relationships and societal structures, the silent threads of inherited family trauma weave through generations, often unnoticed yet profoundly influential. As we delve into the concept of trauma-informed communities, we recognize that these are not merely clusters of individuals but ecosystems of interconnected lives, where the health and resilience of one part invariably affect the whole.

A trauma-informed community acknowledges the pervasive impact of trauma and understands potential paths for recovery. It recognizes the signs and symptoms of trauma in individuals, families, and groups. It integrates this knowledge into its practices and policies. In doing so, it actively seeks to resist re-traumatization and to foster a supportive environment where healing can occur.

The foundation of such a community lies in empathy and education. Empathy, the ability to understand and share the feelings of another, is the cornerstone of a trauma-informed approach. It requires us to look beyond individuals' immediate behaviors and circumstances and consider the complex interplay of historical, emotional, and psychological factors that contribute to their current state.

Education, on the other hand, equips community members with the knowledge to recognize the signs of inherited trauma. It enables them to respond appropriately, whether it be through providing support, advocating for resources, or simply offering a listening ear. Education also serves to destigmatize the experiences of those affected by trauma, fostering a culture of openness and acceptance.

In practice, a trauma-informed community operates on several principles. Safety is paramount—both physical and emotional. People need to feel secure before they can begin to address the wounds of the past. Trustworthiness is also crucial, as it lays the groundwork for meaningful connections and the belief that change is possible.

Collaboration and mutuality are the lifeblood of a trauma-informed community. Healing from trauma is rarely a solitary journey; it thrives on the mutual support and shared experiences of others. Empowerment, voice, and choice are also essential, as they restore a sense of control and agency to those who may feel dispossessed by their inherited burdens.

In such communities, service providers and community leaders are not to act as distant authorities but as healing facilitators. They empower individuals and families, helping them navigate the complexities of their experiences and find their own paths to wellness. This approach requires a shift from asking "What's wrong with you?" to

"What happened to you?"—a subtle yet profound change in perspective that honors the individual's story and strength.

Moreover, trauma-informed communities are proactive in their approach to intergenerational healing. They invest in programs and initiatives that address the root causes of trauma, such as poverty, discrimination, and violence. They also strive to create opportunities for positive experiences and relationships that can counterbalance the effects of past traumas.

The ripple effect of such an approach is far-reaching. When a community becomes trauma-informed, it not only aids in the healing of those directly affected by inherited family trauma but also contributes to the overall well-being of all its members. It becomes a place where cycles of pain are interrupted and replaced with cycles of growth and resilience.

As we look towards the horizon of a more compassionate and understanding society, we see the emergence of trauma-informed communities as beacons of hope. They stand as a testament to our collective ability to confront the shadows of the past and to lay the groundwork for a future where the legacy of trauma is acknowledged, addressed, and transformed into a source of collective strength.

Education and Awareness: Breaking the Stigma

Inherited family trauma is not merely a personal struggle; it casts a long shadow across generations, influencing relationships and the very fabric of society. Yet, despite its pervasive nature, there remains a profound stigma attached to the acknowledgment and discussion of such trauma. This stigma acts as a barrier, preventing individuals from seeking the support they need and society from offering the understanding necessary for healing.

Breaking this stigma requires a multifaceted approach, with education and awareness at its core. It is essential to foster a culture where the complexities of inherited trauma are recognized and addressed with compassion rather than judgment. This begins with transforming our educational systems to include comprehensive mental health education that encompasses the nuances of inherited trauma.

By integrating this topic into school curriculums, we can equip the next generation with a better understanding of the psychological and emotional legacies that can be passed down through families. This education should not only focus on the symptoms and mechanisms of inherited trauma but also emphasize resilience, coping strategies, and the importance of seeking help. Such an approach can empower young people to break cycles of trauma, fostering healthier relationships and communities.

Moreover, awareness campaigns play a pivotal role in changing public perception. These campaigns should aim to normalize conversations about mental health and inherited trauma, highlighting personal stories and scientific research. By bringing these narratives into the public domain, we can challenge misconceptions and create a more empathetic society that encourages healing and support.

Healthcare professionals also have a significant role in breaking the stigma. Training for doctors, therapists, and social workers should include modules on the identification and treatment of inherited trauma. A well-informed healthcare provider can offer appropriate support and validate a patient's experiences, which is a crucial step in destigmatizing the issue.

In addition to formal education and professional training, the media has a powerful influence on public opinion. Responsible reporting and storytelling can contribute to a more informed and sensitive portrayal of inherited trauma. Media professionals should be encouraged to engage with experts and those affected by inherited trauma to ensure that their stories are told with accuracy and dignity.

Breaking the stigma surrounding inherited family trauma is not an overnight task. It requires a concerted effort from educators, healthcare providers, policymakers, the media, and society. By fostering an environment of openness and education, we can create a supportive space for individuals to share their experiences without fear of judgment. In doing so, we pave the way for healing within families and within the broader societal tapestry woven from the threads of our collective experiences.

Policy and Advocacy: Social Change

In the quest to understand inherited family trauma, we have journeyed through the corridors of personal experience and societal perception. We've explored the profound impact that unaddressed trauma can have on individuals and the relationships they nurture. As we turn our attention to the broader societal implications, it becomes clear that the path to healing is not just a private endeavor but a collective one, requiring policy and advocacy to forge social change.

The acknowledgment of inherited family trauma as a significant factor in the well-being of individuals and communities has been slow to permeate the halls of legislation and public policy. Yet, the need for such recognition is critical. Through the lens of policy, society can shift from a reactive stance to a proactive one, implementing strategies that address the symptoms of trauma, its root causes, and intergenerational transmission.

Advocacy plays a pivotal role in this transformation. Advocates for mental health and trauma-informed care are the voices that can articulate the silent struggles of countless individuals, bringing their stories to the forefront of public consciousness. They serve as the bridge between personal narratives and policy-making, translating the complex language of trauma into actionable items that can be enshrined in law and practice.

One of the most significant steps in policy and advocacy is the integration of trauma-informed approaches into all sectors of society. This means training educators, healthcare providers, law enforcement, and social services personnel to recognize the signs of inherited trauma and to respond with empathy and effective interventions. It requires a shift in perspective from punitive measures to supportive ones, recognizing that behaviors often stem from cycles of trauma.

Moreover, policy initiatives must provide accessible and affordable mental health resources to all population segments. This includes funding for research into the effects of inherited trauma and the development of targeted therapies to halt the cycle. It also involves creating community-based programs that offer support and education to families dealing with the repercussions of past traumas.

In advocating for these changes, it is essential to engage with those who have lived experiences of inherited trauma. Their insights are invaluable in shaping well-informed but also compassionate and effective policies. Policies that genuinely resonate with the needs of those they are meant to serve can be crafted by involving survivors in the conversation.

Furthermore, policy and advocacy must also address the broader societal conditions that perpetuate trauma. This includes tackling systemic issues such as poverty, discrimination, and violence, which can all contribute to the cycle of trauma within families. By creating a more equitable and just society, we reduce the stressors that exacerbate inherited trauma and create an environment where healing can flourish.

The journey toward social change is undoubtedly complex, but it is also filled with hope. Each policy enacted, each advocate who raises their voice, and each professionally trained in trauma-informed care contributes to a society that not only recognizes the deep-seated impact of inherited family trauma but also commits to healing it. Through these collective efforts, we can envision a future where the ripple effect of trauma is met with a tide of support, understanding, and transformation—a legacy of healing that benefits not just individuals and families but society as a whole.

Creating a Legacy of Healing

In the wake of understanding how policy and advocacy can be leveraged to address the widespread impact of inherited family trauma, we find ourselves at a crossroads of personal responsibility and collective healing. The journey from recognizing the existence of such trauma to actively engaging in the creation of a legacy of healing is both intimate and communal. The path demands courage, compassion, and a deep commitment to transformation.

Creating a legacy of healing begins within the intricate web of our relationships. It is in the day-to-day interactions with family, friends, and partners that the patterns of inherited trauma often reveal themselves. These patterns, woven into the fabric of our interactions, can either perpetuate pain cycles or become the threads from which we weave a tapestry of recovery.

To embark on this transformative journey, we must cultivate a profound self-awareness. This involves a willingness to delve into past narratives, hold them up to the light of our consciousness, and discern the threads of trauma that may be influencing our present behaviors and choices. It is not an easy task; it requires vulnerability and a willingness to confront uncomfortable truths. Yet, through this process, we can begin to untangle the knots of our inherited stories and reclaim the agency to write new chapters.

As we engage in this personal work, we must also focus on the societal structures that hold these traumas in place. Healing is not solely an individual endeavor but inextricably linked to the collective. The environments in which we live, work, and play all contribute to either the perpetuation or the healing of inherited trauma. By advocating for compassionate and trauma-informed practices within our communities and institutions, we can create spaces that acknowledge the pain of the past and foster resilience and healing.

Moreover, the act of healing is not a solitary one. It thrives in the presence of empathetic witnesses who can hold space for our stories without judgment. This means building connections rooted in mutual respect, active listening, and emotional support in relationships. Through these relationships, we can find the strength to confront our inherited traumas and the support to navigate the complex journey of healing.

As we forge these bonds, we must also be mindful of the legacy we wish to leave for future generations. The choices we make, how we heal, and the relationships we nurture all have the potential to either reinforce the cycle of trauma or break it. By consciously choosing to heal, we are transforming our lives and shaping the inheritance we pass on to our children and their children after them.

In creating a legacy of healing, we are tasked with envisioning a future where the scars of the past no longer dictate the possibilities of the present. It is a future where each individual has the opportunity to thrive, unburdened by the weight of unspoken histories. It is a future built on the foundation of healed relationships and a society that values the wholeness of every person.

The work of healing inherited family trauma is both a personal journey and a societal imperative. It is a process that unfolds over time, with each step forward contributing to a more significant movement towards wholeness. As we engage in this work, we are reclaiming our own lives and contributing to creating a more compassionate and resilient world. It is a profound responsibility and a profound gift—a legacy of healing that can ripple through generations, transforming pain into purpose and despair into hope.

Chapter Summary

- Inherited family trauma can subtly influence interpersonal relationships, affecting behavior and emotional responses across generations.
- Trauma patterns can manifest in nonverbal cues and emotional reactions, often transmitted through unspoken languages within families.
- These inherited patterns can lead to dysfunctional relationship cycles, normalizing harmful behaviors due to familiarity.
- Recognizing inherited trauma patterns is crucial for breaking the cycle, fostering empathy, and beginning the healing process.
- Healing involves developing new emotional vocabularies and may require therapeutic interventions to address the complexities of inherited trauma.

- Trauma-informed communities acknowledge the impact of trauma and integrate this understanding into their practices and policies, fostering a supportive environment for healing.
- Education and awareness campaigns are crucial to breaking the stigma around inherited family trauma, normalizing discussions, and promoting understanding.
- Policy and advocacy are essential for societal change, requiring the integration of trauma-informed approaches across sectors and addressing systemic issues that perpetuate trauma.

10

THE NEXT GENERATION: PARENTING WITH AWARENESS

Conscious Parenting: Breaking the Cycle

In the journey of parenting, the concept of consciousness extends far beyond a child's immediate physical and emotional needs. It delves into the profound responsibility of nurturing a future adult who is not only resilient but also psychologically sound. This task becomes particularly challenging when parents themselves are the bearers of inherited family trauma. The shadows of the past, often silent and unseen, can stretch out their fingers to touch the lives of the next generation in subtle and profound ways.

Breaking the cycle of inherited family trauma is akin to tending a garden that has been neglected; it requires patience, understanding, and a willingness to delve into the soil of one's own experiences. Conscious parenting is being present with one's children, but it is also about being present with oneself. It is about recognizing the patterns handed down, perhaps through generations, and deliberately choosing not to pass them on.

To embark on this journey, parents must first acknowledge the existence of these patterns. It is not uncommon for individuals to carry the emotional baggage of their ancestors without realizing it. These can manifest as fears, anxieties, and reactions that seem disproportionate to the events that trigger them. By identifying these echoes from the past, parents can begin to understand how their behavior might be influenced by unresolved trauma.

Once acknowledged, the process of healing can begin. This is not a journey that one can undertake alone; it often requires the support of professionals who can guide and facilitate the healing process. Therapy, support groups, and other resources can provide the tools necessary to unpack the weight of the past. As parents work through their traumas, they become more capable of providing their children with a stable and nurturing environment.

But conscious parenting is not just about healing old wounds; it's also about fostering an environment where new, healthy patterns can emerge. This involves creating a space where children feel safe to express their emotions and where those emotions are met with empathy and understanding. It is about setting firm yet flexible boundaries, providing structure without stifling the child's individuality.

In this nurturing space, children learn to recognize and articulate their feelings. They are allowed to develop emotional intelligence, which is the ability to be aware of, control, and express their emotions and handle interpersonal relationships judiciously and empathetically.

This skill is invaluable, laying the foundation for a lifetime of healthy relationships and emotional well-being.

Conscious parenting also requires a commitment to self-reflection. Parents must be willing to look at their responses and consider how their histories might influence them. It is a practice of asking oneself, "Is my reaction to my child's behavior about what they are doing now, or is it a response to something that happened in my past?" By staying mindful of these distinctions, parents can respond to their children in ways that are appropriate to the present moment rather than being colored by the past.

In breaking the cycle of inherited family trauma, parents give their children a precious gift: the chance to live a life that is not predetermined by the pains of previous generations. The path requires courage and commitment, but the rewards are immeasurable. Not only does it free the child to forge their path, but it also allows the parent to heal and grow in ways they may never have thought possible.

As we move forward, it is essential to consider how the principles of conscious parenting can be applied to foster attachment and emotional intelligence. These are the cornerstones upon which children can build a life that is not only free from the burdens of the past but also rich in emotional depth and understanding.

Attachment and Emotional Intelligence

During the delicate process of raising children, the silent echoes of the past often reverberate through the generations, manifesting as inherited family trauma. The imprints of these ancestral echoes can shape the emotional landscape of the next generation, often without conscious awareness. As we navigate the delicate terrain of raising children, we must foster secure attachments and cultivate emotional intelligence, both of which serve as bulwarks against the perpetuation of familial wounds.

Attachment, the deep and enduring emotional bond that connects one person to another across time and space, is the cornerstone of a child's early development. Through this primal connection, a child learns to perceive the world as either a safe haven or a landscape fraught with unpredictability. Parents attuned to their children's needs, who respond with warmth and consistency, lay the groundwork for secure attachment. This secure base is not merely a sanctuary of comfort but also a launching pad from which children can explore their environment with confidence and curiosity.

However, for parents who have themselves been the bearers of inherited trauma, the capacity to provide this secure base can be compromised. Their attachment histories, possibly marred by the shadows of unresolved pain, can inadvertently color their attachment styles to their children. It is here that the cycle of trauma finds its potential perpetuation. Yet, it is also here that the cycle can be interrupted.

Emotional intelligence, the ability to understand and manage one's emotions, as well as to empathize with the emotions of others, is a beacon that guides this interruption. Parents who consciously work on developing their emotional intelligence are better equipped to recognize and regulate their emotional responses. They can discern the subtle difference between reacting from a place of historical hurt and responding from a place of present-moment awareness.

By cultivating emotional intelligence, parents can model for their children how to navigate the complex tapestry of human emotions. Children, in turn, learn to articulate their feelings, understand the emotional cues of others, and develop empathy. This emotional literacy becomes the language through which they can communicate their inner worlds, build meaningful relationships, and engage with life's challenges with resilience.

Moreover, emotional intelligence allows parents to hold space for their children's emotions without being overwhelmed by their own. It enables them to approach their children's distress with compassion rather than anxiety, curiosity, and control. In doing so, they offer their children a relationship where emotions are not feared but are understood as signals, as messengers of needs and desires.

As we embark on parenting with awareness, we are not merely raising children but nurturing the seeds of emotional health that will flourish for generations to come. We are rewriting the narrative of our lineage, transforming inherited trauma into inherited wisdom. In this transformation lies the hope for our children to live lives unencumbered by the weight of the past, empowered to craft their own stories with intention and grace.

Teaching Resilience and Coping Skills

On the gentle path of raising children, the awareness of inherited family trauma serves as a compass, guiding us toward nurturing environments that foster resilience and equip our children with practical coping skills. As we delve into the heart of this nurturing, it is essential to understand that the ability to bounce back from adversity is not an innate trait but a skill that can be cultivated and strengthened over time.

Resilience is often misconstrued as a stoic endurance of hardship. Still, in its essence, it is the graceful dance of adapting to change, recovering from setbacks, and learning from each experience. It is about developing a core of inner strength that can be drawn upon in times of need. To instill this quality in the next generation, we must first embody it ourselves, for children are astute observers, learning more from what they witness than what they are told.

One of the most profound ways to teach resilience is through modeling. When parents face their challenges with hope and a problem-solving mindset, they provide a live blueprint for their children to emulate. It is not the absence of struggle that is most instructive but how we navigate it. By sharing our thought processes, embracing our emotions, and demonstrating perseverance, we communicate to our children that difficulties are a part of life and that they possess the capacity to overcome them.

Coping skills are the tools and strategies that individuals use to manage stress and emotional upheaval. These skills are as varied as the individuals who employ them. Yet, certain practices have been universally shown to be effective. Mindfulness, for instance, is a practice that roots us in the present moment and allows us to observe our thoughts and feelings without judgment. By teaching our children mindfulness, we give them the gift of self-awareness, which is the first step in emotional regulation.

Another vital coping skill is emotional expression. Encouraging children to articulate their feelings through conversation, art, or play helps them process their emotions. It reduces the likelihood of these feelings manifesting in harmful ways. Parents need to create a safe space where emotions are not only allowed but welcomed. This openness paves the way for children to seek support and guidance when struggling rather than bottling up their feelings.

Problem-solving is a skill that empowers children to take active steps in confronting their challenges. Children learn that they have agency in their lives by breaking down problems into manageable pieces, considering various solutions, and evaluating outcomes. Parents can foster this skill by involving their children in discussions about family challenges, allowing them to offer input and, when appropriate, letting them experience the natural consequences of their choices.

In addition to these practices, it is crucial to recognize the role of social support in building resilience. Relationships with family, friends, and community members provide a network of care that can buffer against the effects of stress and trauma. Teaching children to cultivate and maintain these relationships ensures they can access diverse perspectives and resources when facing challenges.

As we journey forward, it is with the understanding that resilience and coping skills are not static qualities but dynamic processes that evolve with experience. Our role as parents is not to shield our children from every hardship but to prepare them to meet life's complexities with courage, adaptability, and an open heart. In doing so, we help to break the cycle of inherited family trauma, paving the way for a future where each generation is stronger and more emotionally intelligent than the last.

The Role of Education and Support

As we navigate the complex landscape of parenting in the shadow of inherited family trauma, it becomes increasingly clear that education and support play pivotal roles in shaping the future of the next generation. The task at hand is not only to break the cycle of trauma but to nurture an environment where children can thrive, unencumbered by the burdens of the past.

To this end, parents need to seek out and engage with educational resources that provide insight into the nature of inherited trauma. Knowledge is a powerful tool in this journey. Understanding how trauma can be transmitted across generations enables parents to identify patterns that may be present in their family history. This awareness is the first step toward change.

However, education extends beyond the theoretical understanding of trauma. It involves learning practical strategies for creating a stable and nurturing home environment. Parenting programs and workshops can offer valuable guidance on fostering secure attachment, emotional intelligence, and open communication. These skills empower parents to become the architects of a new family legacy that champions emotional health and resilience.

Support systems are equally crucial. The journey of healing and transformation can be arduous and lonely without a network of understanding individuals who can offer empathy, encouragement, and advice. Support groups, whether in-person or online, provide a communal space for parents to share experiences, challenges, and triumphs. Within these groups, parents often find solace in the shared understanding that they are not alone in their struggles.

Moreover, professional support from therapists or counselors trained in dealing with family trauma can be instrumental. These professionals can guide parents through the process of unpacking their trauma, learning how to manage its impact, and developing strategies to prevent its transmission to their children. They can also assist in addressing any signs of trauma that may already be manifesting in children, providing early intervention that can alter the course of a child's life.

It is essential to recognize that education and support are not static resources but dynamic processes that evolve as a family grows and changes. As children develop, new challenges and questions arise, necessitating a continuous commitment to learning and seeking support. This ongoing engagement is a testament to the resilience of the human spirit and its capacity for growth and transformation.

In the context of inherited family trauma, the role of education and support is not merely to inform or to console—it is to empower. It is to equip parents with the tools they need to rewrite the narratives of their lives and, in doing so, to lay the groundwork for their children to build their own stories, free from the echoes of trauma. This empowerment is the foundation upon which hope and positive futures are built, ensuring that the legacy passed down to the next generation is one of strength, understanding, and boundless potential.

Fostering Hope and Positive Futures

In the delicate dance of parenting, the awareness of inherited family trauma is akin to a subtle undercurrent that can guide the steps of those involved. It is a silent narrative that, if left unaddressed, can repeat its patterns through generations. However, when parents approach their role with a conscious understanding of this phenomenon, they can change the rhythm and foster hope and positive futures for their children.

The task is not to eradicate the past—our histories are indelible parts of us—but to cultivate an environment where the past does not dictate the future. It is about nurturing resilience and equipping the next generation with the tools to survive and thrive despite the shadows that may loom from familial experiences.

To achieve this, parents can adopt a proactive stance that emphasizes the strengths and potential of their children. This involves recognizing each child as an individual separate from the family's traumatic narrative. It is about celebrating their unique qualities and encouraging their personal growth and development, free from the constraints of inherited burdens.

Creating open lines of communication is paramount. Children should feel safe to express their emotions, fears, and dreams. By fostering a household where dialogue about feelings and experiences is normalized, parents can help their children develop emotional intelligence and resilience. This practice also serves as a preventive measure, ensuring that children do not internalize stress or trauma as their predecessors might have.

Moreover, instilling a sense of hope and optimism in children is essential. This can be achieved through positive reinforcement, highlighting their achievements, and supporting their ambitions. It is also important to model coping strategies emphasizing adaptability and problem-solving, showing children that challenges can be met with creativity and determination.

In addition, parents can encourage their children to engage with the world around them, fostering connections with peers, mentors, and communities. These relationships can provide support systems outside of the family unit, offering diverse perspectives and experiences that can enrich a child's worldview and sense of belonging.

Lastly, parents need to engage in self-care and personal development. By addressing their traumas and emotional needs, parents can break the transmission cycle and present a healthier model of coping and living for their children to emulate. This self-work is not a selfish act but a profound investment in the well-being of future generations.

In conclusion, parenting with awareness of inherited family trauma is a journey that requires intention, compassion, and a forward-looking perspective. It is about creating a legacy not of repeated patterns but of conscious growth and healing. By fostering hope and optimistic futures, parents can empower their children to write stories that honor the past but are not bound by it.

Chapter Summary

- Conscious parenting involves nurturing a psychologically sound future adult and breaking the cycle of inherited family trauma.
- Parents must acknowledge and understand their inherited patterns to prevent passing them on to their children.
- Healing from inherited trauma often requires professional support, such as therapy, to provide a stable environment for children.
- Conscious parenting includes creating a safe space for emotional expression and fostering emotional intelligence in children.
- Parents need to practice self-reflection to ensure their reactions to their children are present-focused and not influenced by past trauma.
- Secure attachment and emotional intelligence are crucial to preventing the perpetuation of familial wounds and fostering resilience.
- Education and support systems, including parenting programs and professional counseling, are crucial for parents dealing with inherited trauma.
- Fostering hope and positive futures involves recognizing each child's individuality, open communication, and parents' self-care and personal development.

EMBRACING OUR COLLECTIVE JOURNEY

Reflecting on Our Shared Humanity

As we draw near the close of this exploration into the depths of inherited family trauma, it is essential to pause and consider the profound interconnectedness that binds us all. The tapestry of our lives is woven with threads of experiences passed down through generations, each strand colored with the hues of joy, pain, resilience, and hope. Recognizing our shared humanity, we find the strength to confront the shadows of our collective past and the courage to illuminate the path forward.

Inherited trauma is not a solitary journey. It is a shared narrative that crosses the boundaries of time, culture, and geography. The silent echo of our ancestors' struggles resonates within us, shaping our beliefs, behaviors, and the essence of our being. Yet, within this echo lies a universal truth: we are more alike than different. Our capacity to feel pain and heal is a testament to the indomitable spirit that resides within us.

As we reflect on the stories that have been shared, the insights gleaned, and the wisdom imparted, we understand that acknowledging our vulnerabilities is not a sign of weakness but a courageous act of authenticity. Through this vulnerability, we invite connection, understanding, and healing. By recognizing the fragments of ourselves in the experiences of others, we begin to dismantle the barriers that have kept us isolated in our suffering.

The journey of healing inherited family trauma is not one that we undertake alone. It is a collective endeavor that requires us to extend our hands in solidarity, to offer our shoulders for others to lean on, and to open our hearts to the stories that have shaped us. It is a process that demands empathy, not just for others but for ourselves, for it is in the gentle embrace of self-compassion that we find the space to grow, change, and break the cycles that have held us captive.

In embracing our shared humanity, we recognize that the path to healing is not linear. It is a mosaic of experiences, a constellation of moments with the potential for growth and transformation. We learn to celebrate the small victories, cherish the incremental steps toward wholeness, and honor the resilience that has carried us through the darkest times.

As we stand at the precipice of new beginnings, let us carry with us the knowledge that our stories do not end with us. They ripple outwards, touching the lives of those yet to come. It is our responsibility, our privilege, to pave the way for a future where the chains of inherited trauma are broken and where the next generation can flourish unencumbered by the weight of the past.

In the stillness of introspection, let us hold space for the healing yet to unfold, the stories yet to be told, and the collective journey that we continue to navigate. Together, with compassion as our compass and empathy as our guide, we step into a world where our shared humanity is the beacon that lights the way to a brighter, more connected future.

The Power of Compassion and Empathy

As we conclude our exploration of inherited family trauma, we come to recognize a profound truth: the healing journey is not one we walk alone. It is a path paved with the collective efforts of every individual who dares to confront the echoes of the past. In this recognition, we find the power of compassion and empathy to be therapeutic tools and vital human connections that bind us in our quest for understanding and peace.

Compassion, in its purest form, is an emotional response that arises from witnessing another's suffering, coupled with a genuine desire to alleviate it. When we apply compassion to inherited family trauma, we extend our hearts to those who came before us and ourselves and our descendants. It is an acknowledgment that the wounds we carry are not singular in their existence; they are shared across generations, and thus, our compassion must be expansive and inclusive.

Empathy, the ability to understand and share the feelings of another, is the bridge that connects our own experiences with those of our ancestors. Empathy allows us to feel the weight of their stories and acknowledge the burden of their unhealed traumas without judgment or reservation. Through this empathetic connection, we begin to unravel the complex tapestry of our family's emotional legacy.

The power of these twin forces—compassion and empathy—lies in their ability to transform our perspective. They encourage us to look beyond the surface of our inherited narratives to see the vulnerabilities and strengths passed down through time. They ask us to consider the resilience of the human spirit and the capacity for renewal that resides within each of us.

In embracing compassion and empathy, we also embrace a form of radical acceptance. This acceptance does not mean condoning the painful events of the past or the behaviors that arose from them. Instead, it is an acknowledgment of their reality, an understanding that to move forward, we must first accept where we are and where we have come from. It is a gentle but firm assertion that we are not defined by our trauma but by how we respond to it.

As we cultivate these qualities within ourselves, we also foster a more compassionate and empathetic society. We become advocates for healing within the confines of our own families and within the broader human family. We recognize that the threads of trauma are interwoven in the fabric of our collective history and that by pulling on one, we have the chance to unravel them all.

In this space of shared vulnerability and mutual support, we find the courage to confront the shadows of the past. We learn to hold space for each other's stories, to listen deeply, and to respond with kindness. Here, in the heart of compassion and empathy, we discover the potential for profound transformation—not as isolated individuals but as a united community bound by the common threads of our human experience.

As we stand on the threshold of this understanding, we prepare to step into the wisdom of healing, carrying with us the lessons of compassion and empathy as guiding lights on our collective journey.

The Wisdom of Healing

As we approach the end of our exploration into the depths of inherited family trauma, we arrive at a place of profound understanding—a place where the wisdom of healing begins to illuminate our path. This wisdom, often hard-earned through the trials of personal experience and collective suffering, offers a beacon of hope that guides us toward a future less burdened by the echoes of our ancestors' pain.

The journey of healing is not a solitary one. It is a tapestry woven from the threads of our shared humanity, colored by the diverse experiences we bring to the loom. In recognizing the interconnectedness of our stories, we find strength. It is a strength that comes not from isolation but from the collective courage to face the shadows of our familial pasts and the determination to transform them into the light for future generations.

Healing inherited family trauma requires us to delve into the innermost chambers of our hearts to confront the fears and vulnerabilities that reside there. It is a process that demands honesty, not just with ourselves but also our lineage. As we embark on this introspective journey, we learn that the wisdom of healing is not about erasing the past but about understanding its influence on our present and reshaping its impact on our future.

This wisdom teaches us that healing is an act of reclamation. It is about reclaiming our narratives, our identities, and our rightful place within the continuum of our family's history. It is about acknowledging the suffering that has been endured while also recognizing the resilience that has allowed us to survive and, indeed, to thrive. Through this reclamation, we begin to dissolve the barriers that trauma has erected between us and our potential for growth and fulfillment.

The wisdom of healing also brings with it the recognition that we are not just the sum of our inherited pain. We also carry our ancestors' dreams, hopes, and unfulfilled aspirations. In healing, we honor their legacy not by perpetuating their traumas but by nurturing the seeds of possibility they planted, often unconsciously, within us. We become the custodians of a new legacy—one defined by healing, empowerment, and the promise of a future unshackled from the chains of the past.

As we embrace this wisdom, we find that the healing process is not linear. It ebbs and flows like the tides, with moments of profound insight and periods of quiet reflection. Each step forward is an act of bravery, a testament to the human spirit's capacity for renewal and transformation. And with each step, we weave a new pattern into the fabric of our lives, one that honors the complexity of our heritage while forging a path toward a more conscious and compassionate existence.

In this space of healing, we are not alone. We stand shoulder to shoulder with those who have walked this path before us and those who will follow in our footsteps. Together, we are part of a collective journey that transcends time and space, uniting us in a shared quest for understanding, peace, and a world where the wisdom of healing is not just an aspiration but a reality for all.

The Horizon of Possibility

As we stand on the precipice of understanding, gazing into the vast expanse of what could be, we must recognize the power of possibility that lies before us. The journey of grappling with inherited family trauma is not a path walked in isolation. It is a collective expedition that we navigate together as a society enriched by diverse experiences and united by a common desire for healing and growth.

The horizon of possibility stretches out, inviting us to envision a future where the chains of intergenerational pain are acknowledged and actively dismantled. It is a future where the narratives of our ancestors become lessons of resilience rather than scripts for suffering. In this envisioned world, the wisdom gleaned from our forebears' trials is transformed into a roadmap for emotional liberation and well-being.

Imagine a society that embraces the complexity of its history, where the stories of our lineage are not sources of shame but wellsprings of strength. In this society, children are born into environments conscious of the past but not confined by it. Parents and guardians are equipped with the tools to not only heal their wounds but also to prevent the transmission of trauma to the next generation.

The science of epigenetics has shown us that our genes are not our destiny. They are dynamic and responsive to the environments we create and the experiences we undergo. This knowledge empowers us to be architects of our genetic expression and to choose paths of healing that can reverberate through our DNA and echo into the lives of our descendants.

As we look forward, we must also look inward, recognizing that the journey of healing is as much about personal transformation as it is about collective change. It is about cultivating empathy for ourselves and those who came before us, understanding that they, too, were products of their time, often doing their best with the knowledge and resources available to them.

The horizon of possibility is not a distant dream but a tangible destination we can reach through conscious effort and societal commitment. It requires us to be both students and teachers, learning from the past and educating for the future. It asks us to be courageous, confront uncomfortable truths, and embrace the vulnerability that comes with genuine healing.

In this potential space, we find the seeds of a new narrative that honors our history without being hindered by it. It is a narrative that celebrates growth, champions resilience, and fosters a culture of emotional intelligence and psychological well-being.

As we close this chapter of our collective journey, let us implement the lessons learned optimistically. Let us commit to nurturing these seeds of possibility, watering them with our collective efforts, and watching as they blossom into a legacy of healing that will benefit future generations. The horizon is vast, and it is ours to shape.

What We Leave Behind

In the quiet afterglow of reflection, as we stand on the precipice of understanding and the dawn of healing, we are beckoned to consider the trajectory of our lives and the legacy we impart to those who follow. The journey through the pages of this exploration into inherited family trauma has been one of unraveling threads that weave through generations, binding us in a tapestry of shared history and collective memory.

We have delved into the shadows cast by our ancestors, not to dwell in the darkness but to bring light to the patterns that have shaped us. We have learned that trauma, when left unacknowledged, can echo through time, manifesting in the lives of those who were never present at its inception. Yet, with this knowledge comes a profound responsibility—a call to action that asks us to be the architects of a new legacy.

What we leave behind is a consequence of our actions and our conscious choices. It is a testament to the understanding that the wounds we heal in ourselves can mend fractures in the lineage we continue. As we step forward, let us do so to transform our inherited pain into wisdom, our silent struggles into dialogues of growth, and our healing into collective liberation.

To embark on this path requires courage—the courage to confront uncomfortable truths, to challenge long-held beliefs, and to open ourselves to the vulnerability of change. It demands that we be both students and teachers in life's lessons, recognizing that every interaction is an opportunity to either perpetuate cycles of suffering or foster cycles of healing.

Let us nurture resilience over resignation, empathy over apathy, and connection over isolation. In doing so, we honor those who came before us and those who will follow. Our actions today are the seeds of tomorrow's harvest, and it is within our power to cultivate a future where the legacy of trauma is replaced with triumph over adversity.

As we close this chapter of our collective journey, let us not forget that the story continues with each breath we take and every choice we make. The call to action is clear: to live with intention, to love with purpose, and to leave a legacy that echoes with the strength of healed hearts and the whispers of a brighter future for all who inherit the world we shape today.

HOW TO DEAL WITH EMOTIONALLY IMMATURE PARENTS

HEALING FROM NARCISSISTIC, AUTHORITARIAN, PERMISSIVE, ENMESHED, OR ABSENT PARENTS

UNDERSTANDING EMOTIONAL IMMATURITY

The Landscape of Emotional Immaturity

In the realm of family dynamics, emotional immaturity in parents is a phenomenon that, while often unspoken, casts long shadows across their children's lives. It is a landscape marked by behaviors and attitudes that, at their core, reveal a stunted development in emotional regulation, empathy, and self-awareness. These parents may not necessarily lack love or good intentions for their children. Still, their emotional responses can be unpredictable, self-centered, or childish, leading to a confusing and sometimes painful upbringing.

It is essential to recognize the various contours that define emotional immaturity to navigate this landscape. These parents may exhibit a limited emotional vocabulary, often struggling to articulate their feelings or understand the emotional cues of others. Their reactions to stress can be impulsive, and they might prioritize their emotional needs over those of their children. This can manifest in dismissive, intrusive, or even neglectful behaviors, depending on the situation at hand.

A lack of consistent nurturing and support often characterizes the emotional climate created by such parents. Children in these environments might find themselves playing the caretaker role as they learn to manage their own emotions and those of their parents. This role reversal can lead to an accelerated loss of childhood innocence as children are compelled to navigate adult emotions and responsibilities prematurely.

Moreover, emotionally immature parents may struggle with boundaries, either being overly enmeshed with their children or, conversely, detached and uninvolved. This inconsistency can leave children feeling insecure and unsure about their place in the family and the world. They might grapple with guilt for desiring independence or harbor resentment for the emotional labor they've been shouldered.

Understanding the landscape of emotional immaturity in parents is crucial in recognizing the patterns and impacts of such upbringing. It is a terrain that requires careful navigation, for the echoes of childhood experiences can resonate well into adulthood. As we delve deeper into the nuances of emotional immaturity, we can unravel the complex tapestry of behaviors and motivations that shape these parental relationships, paving the way for healing and growth for both parents and their children.

Defining Emotional Immaturity in Parents

Emotional maturity refers to the ability to manage and understand one's emotions, engage with others in empathetic and considerate ways, and navigate relationships' complexities with a sense of responsibility and foresight. Conversely, emotional immaturity in parents manifests as a chronic pattern of emotional responses that are more aligned with those of a much younger individual, often marked by impulsivity, self-centeredness, and a limited capacity for empathy.

Emotionally immature parents may struggle to provide the emotional support and stability that children require for healthy development. This immaturity does not necessarily stem from a lack of love or concern for their offspring. Instead, it is indicative of an underdeveloped emotional skill set. These parents may have difficulty processing their own emotions maturely, which can lead to a range of challenging behaviors for both themselves and their children.

One of the hallmarks of emotional immaturity is a tendency to prioritize one's needs and feelings over those of others. In the context of parenting, this can translate into a lack of attunement to a child's emotional needs. An emotionally immature parent may react to their child's expressions of feelings with dismissal, irritation, or even mockery. Such responses can leave children feeling misunderstood and unsupported and may instill a sense of emotional isolation.

Another characteristic of emotional immaturity is poor emotional regulation. Parents who have not developed this skill may exhibit mood swings, explosive anger, or passive-aggressive behavior. These unpredictable emotional responses can create an environment of instability and anxiety for children, who thrive on consistency and predictability from their caregivers.

Furthermore, emotionally immature parents may struggle with boundaries, either being overly rigid and authoritarian or, conversely, too permissive, failing to set appropriate limits for behavior. This inconsistency can confuse children who benefit from clear and consistent guidelines. Without these, children may struggle to develop self-discipline and an understanding of acceptable social behavior.

It is also worth noting that emotional immaturity is not always constant. Parents may exhibit mature emotional responses in certain situations while reverting to immature patterns in others. This inconsistency can be particularly disorienting for children, who may find it difficult to predict how their parents will react at any given time.

Understanding the nature of emotional immaturity in parents is the first step toward addressing its effects within the family unit. It is a complex issue requiring compassion and insight to navigate successfully. As we delve deeper into the impact of emotional immaturity on family dynamics in the following discussions, we will explore the challenges it presents and the pathways to growth and healing for both parents and children.

The Impact on Family Dynamics

The impact of emotionally immature parents on family dynamics is profound and multifaceted. Children raised in such environments often find themselves in the paradoxical position of having to navigate the unpredictable emotional landscapes of their caregivers while simultaneously striving to develop their sense of stability and self-worth.

One of the most significant consequences is the role reversal that can occur within the family structure. Children may find themselves stepping into the caretaker role, providing emotional support, or managing household responsibilities beyond their years. This premature thrust into adult-like duties can lead to losing childhood innocence and the necessary space to explore and understand their emotions and needs.

Moreover, the emotional development of these children can be stunted as they mirror the immature emotional responses they observe. They may struggle with expressing their feelings appropriately or understanding the emotional cues of others, which can lead to difficulties in forming healthy relationships outside the family unit.

The communication patterns within a family headed by emotionally immature parents can also be significantly affected. Such parents may avoid open discussions about feelings, preferring to sweep issues under the rug or react with volatility rather than engage in constructive dialogue. This can create an environment where children feel unheard and invalidated, fostering a sense of isolation and confusion about effectively communicating their thoughts and emotions.

Furthermore, the unpredictability of an emotionally immature parent's reactions can instill a sense of chronic anxiety in children. They may walk on eggshells, constantly vigilant and trying to anticipate their parents' mood swings or irrational behavior. This hyperawareness can lead to excessive stress and an inability to relax and feel safe within the home environment.

The emotional climate set by immature parents often lacks consistency, which is essential for children to develop a secure attachment style. Without the assurance of a stable, nurturing environment, children may develop insecure or disorganized attachment patterns, affecting their ability to trust and connect with others throughout their lives.

In essence, the impact of emotionally immature parents on family dynamics extends far beyond the immediate family interactions. It can influence children's psychological and emotional well-being long into adulthood, shaping how they perceive themselves, engage with others, and form their own relationships. Within this understanding, we can begin to appreciate the importance of recognizing the signs of emotional immaturity in parents, not only for the benefit of the children involved but for the health of the family unit as a whole.

Recognizing the Signs

In comprehending the complexities of emotional immaturity in parents, it is essential to identify the hallmarks that characterize such behavior. Emotional immaturity can manifest in various ways, often subtle and interwoven into daily interactions, making them challenging to discern. Yet, recognizing these signs is a critical step towards understanding and addressing the issues that arise from being raised by emotionally immature parents.

One of the most telling signs is inconsistency in emotional responses. Emotionally immature parents may react unpredictably to their child's needs or emotions. They might respond with empathy and support one moment, only to be dismissive or even hostile the next. This unpredictability can create a sense of instability and insecurity in children, who learn to tread carefully in the emotional landscape of their home, never quite sure which version of their parent they will encounter.

Another indicator is a tendency towards self-centeredness. Parents with emotional immaturity may prioritize their feelings and needs over their children's. They might seek attention and validation from their child, reversing the typical parent-child dynamic. This self-focus can prevent them from being fully present and attentive to their child's experiences, often leading to a lack of emotional support when the child needs it most.

Difficulty in handling stress and conflict is also a common trait among emotionally immature parents. Instead of approaching challenges with resilience and problem-solving skills, they may become overwhelmed or avoidant. This inability to cope effectively with the everyday stresses of life can leave children feeling alone in navigating their difficulties, as they cannot rely on their parents for guidance or support.

Emotionally immature parents may also struggle with boundaries. They might overshare personal problems or treat their child as a confidant, burdening them with issues that are inappropriate for their age. Conversely, they may be invasive, not respecting their child's privacy or autonomy, hindering their healthy sense of self-development.

Lastly, more emotional depth is often needed. These parents may struggle to engage in deep, meaningful conversations about feelings, dreams, or fears. Their interactions might remain superficial, focused on day-to-day tasks or small talk, leaving their child hungry for a more profound connection that remains unmet.

Recognizing these signs is not about casting blame but gaining insight into the relational patterns that may have shaped one's upbringing. It is the first step in a compassionate journey toward understanding and healing. As we move forward, we will explore how this newfound understanding can set the stage for personal growth and healthier relationships, not just with one's parents but in all areas of life.

Setting the Stage for Healing and Growth

In the journey of understanding our parents and the impact of their emotional immaturity on our lives, recognition is merely the first step. It is akin to turning on a light in a dimly lit room, allowing us to see the contours of the furniture that we've been stumbling over for years. But once we see the obstacles, the question arises: what do we do next? How do we navigate this newfound awareness towards healing and growth?

The process of healing is not linear, nor is it one-size-fits-all. It requires patience, self-compassion, and, often, a reevaluation of the narratives we've held about ourselves and our familial relationships. To set the stage for healing and growth, we must first establish a foundation of understanding—not just our parents' limitations but also our responses.

One of the most profound realizations that can come from recognizing emotional immaturity in parents is the recognition of our survival strategies. As children, we adapt to our environment in ways that allow us to cope with unpredictability and emotional neglect. These adaptations can manifest as hyper-independence, people-pleasing, or an overdeveloped sense of responsibility for others' emotions. While these strategies may have served us in our youth, they can become maladaptive in adulthood, leading to behavior patterns that no longer serve our best interests.

To move forward, it is essential to cultivate an inner dialogue that is both kind and truthful. This means acknowledging the pain and disappointment that come with having emotionally immature parents while also recognizing that we have the power to rewrite our own story. It involves grieving the loss of the parent-child dynamic we may have longed for and, in its place, building an autonomous and resilient sense of self.

Self-care becomes a critical component in setting this stage. It is about creating boundaries that protect our emotional well-being, engaging in activities that nourish us, and seeking out reciprocal and grounding relationships. It is also about learning to parent ourselves in the ways we needed but did not receive. This might include developing emotional regulation skills, practicing self-compassion, and pursuing personal goals that align with our values and aspirations.

Moreover, setting the stage for healing and growth often involves seeking external support. This could come through therapy, support groups, or educational resources that provide insight and validation. It is essential to surround ourselves with individuals who understand the nuanced challenges of having emotionally immature parents and who can offer empathy and guidance as we navigate this complex terrain.

As we embark on this path, it is crucial to remember that healing is not about changing our parents or expecting them to become the figures we need them to be. It is about changing our relationship to our past, taking control of our narrative, and stepping into a future where our emotional well-being is no longer contingent on our capacity for growth.

In this process, we may discover strengths we never knew we had and a capacity for forgiveness and understanding that does not excuse harmful behavior but transcends it. We are not erasing the past by setting the stage for healing and growth. Still, instead, we are permitting ourselves to emerge from its shadow, grow beyond the confines of our upbringing, and cultivate a life rich with emotional maturity and fulfillment.

1

THE ORIGINS OF EMOTIONAL IMMATURITY

Generational Patterns and Legacy

Emotional immaturity in parents is a complex phenomenon that often does not arise in isolation. As we delve into the intricate tapestry of family dynamics, it becomes evident that the roots of such immaturity can frequently be traced back through generations. This legacy of emotional underdevelopment is not merely a repetition of behaviors but a continuation of unaddressed emotional needs and unresolved psychological conflicts.

To understand the generational patterns that contribute to emotional immaturity, it is essential to recognize the role of the family environment in shaping an individual's emotional landscape. Children observe and internalize the emotional responses and coping mechanisms of their caregivers. When parents exhibit emotionally immature behaviors—such as difficulty in handling stress, poor communication skills, or an inability to empathize with others—these traits can become the blueprint for their children's emotional development.

In many cases, emotionally immature parents may have experienced similar deficiencies in their upbringing. Perhaps they were raised in households where emotional expression was discouraged or even punished, suppressing their emotional growth. In such environments, emotions are often viewed as a source of weakness or inconvenience rather than a natural and healthy part of the human experience.

This suppression can create a cycle where emotional expression and healthy emotional regulation are not modeled or taught, leaving children ill-equipped to manage their emotions effectively. As these children grow into adults and become parents themselves, they may struggle with the same emotional limitations that their parents did, perpetuating the cycle.

Moreover, societal and cultural factors can also significantly influence this generational legacy. In some cultures, for example, stoicism is highly valued, and emotional vulnerability is seen as undesirable. Such cultural norms can reinforce the cycle of emotional immaturity, as individuals may feel pressured to conform to these expectations, even when it is detrimental to their emotional well-being.

The impact of historical events on emotional development is also worth considering. Families that have endured trauma, such as war, displacement, or severe economic hardship, may carry the emotional scars of these experiences across generations. The survival mechanisms developed during times of crisis can become ingrained, with emotional openness and vulnerability being sidelined in favor of resilience and self-reliance.

Despite these patterns, it is essential to remember that generational legacies of emotional immaturity are not inescapable destinies. With awareness and effort, individuals can break the cycle. By seeking to understand their emotional heritage and actively working to develop healthier emotional skills, parents can create a new legacy—one that is characterized by emotional maturity and the capacity for deeper, more fulfilling relationships with their children and others.

In recognizing these patterns and their origins, we pave the way for a more compassionate understanding of emotionally immature parents. This understanding is not an excuse for their behaviors but rather a context that can inform the journey toward healing and growth. As we move forward, we will explore the psychological theories that provide further insight into the mechanisms behind emotional immaturity, shedding light on the internal workings of the emotionally underdeveloped mind.

Psychological Theories Behind Emotional Immaturity

In exploring the origins of emotional immaturity in parents, it is essential to delve into the psychological theories that provide a framework for understanding this complex phenomenon. Emotional immaturity can manifest in various behaviors, such as difficulty handling emotions, poor empathy, and a tendency to react rather than respond to challenging situations. These behaviors affect the parents and have profound implications for their children's emotional development.

One of the foundational theories in psychology that sheds light on emotional immaturity is Sigmund Freud's psychoanalytic theory, particularly his concept of the id, ego, and superego. According to Freud, the id is the primitive and instinctual part of the mind that contains sexual and aggressive drives and hidden memories. The superego operates as a moral conscience, and the ego is the realistic part that mediates between the desires of the id and the superego. In the case of emotionally immature parents, there may be an imbalance in these psychic structures, often with a dominant id that drives impulsive, child-like behavior and an underdeveloped superego that fails to temper these impulses with mature moral reasoning.

Another significant theory is Erik Erikson's stages of psychosocial development, which suggests that emotional maturity results from successfully navigating a series of life stages, each with its unique challenge and potential for growth. For some parents, emotional immaturity may stem from difficulties in their developmental stages, resulting in a lack of essential skills such as trust, autonomy, and initiative. These unresolved issues can lead to stagnation and an inability to provide the emotional support and guidance their children need.

Behaviorism, as proposed by John B. Watson and further developed by B.F. Skinner also offers insights into emotional immaturity. This perspective focuses on observable behaviors and how they are learned through interaction with the environment. Emotionally immature parents may have learned maladaptive emotional responses through their experiences and reinforcement histories. They might not have had positive role models to emulate or may have been rewarded for immature behaviors, perpetuating a cycle of emotional underdevelopment.

Cognitive theories, particularly those of Jean Piaget, emphasize the role of mental processes in understanding the world. Piaget's stages of cognitive development highlight how individuals construct a mental model of the world at different ages. Suppose a parent's cognitive development is arrested at a particular stage, perhaps due to trauma or lack of educational opportunities. In that case, they may struggle with abstract thinking or perspective-taking, which is crucial for mature emotional interactions.

Lastly, the humanistic perspective, championed by psychologists such as Carl Rogers and Abraham Maslow, focuses on the individual's capacity for growth and self-actualization. Emotional immaturity in parents might be viewed through this lens as a failure to reach one's potential for psychological growth, often due to conditions not conducive to fostering self-awareness and personal development. These parents may have grown up in environments that did not value or support the exploration of personal emotions and needs, leading to stunted emotional growth.

Understanding these psychological theories provides a backdrop against which we can better comprehend the intricacies of emotional immaturity in parents. It is not a singular issue with a one-size-fits-all explanation but a tapestry woven from various psychological influences and life experiences. As we unravel this tapestry, we will consider how attachment styles, formed early in life, play a pivotal role in shaping the emotional maturity of parents.

The Role of Attachment Styles

Understanding the origins of emotional immaturity in parents often requires us to delve into the complex world of attachment styles. Attachment theory, first developed by John Bowlby and later expanded by Mary Ainsworth, provides a framework for understanding how the bonds formed between children and their caregivers can influence emotional development and behavior later in life.

Attachment styles are bonding patterns that can affect how individuals relate to others, including their own children. These styles are typically categorized as secure, anxious-preoccupied, dismissive-avoidant, and fearful-avoidant. A healthy balance of intimacy and independence characterizes secure attachment. In contrast, the other three styles, known as insecure attachments, can lead to various emotional challenges.

When parents have an insecure attachment style, they may struggle with emotional regulation and interpersonal relationships. For instance, a parent with an anxious-preoccupied attachment may become overly dependent on their child for emotional support, leading to a dynamic where the child feels responsible for the parent's emotional well-being. Conversely, a dismissive-avoidant parent may be emotionally distant, making it difficult for the child to form a close, nurturing bond.

These insecure attachment styles can stem from the parent's own childhood experiences. Suppose they did not receive consistent care and emotional support from their caregivers. In that case, they might not have developed the skills to nurture a secure attachment with their children. This lack of secure attachment can manifest as emotional immaturity, where the parent may be unable to provide the empathy, stability, and responsiveness that their child needs.

Intergenerational patterns can also perpetuate emotional immaturity in parents. Suppose emotionally immature caregivers raised a parent. In that case, they might inadvertently replicate the same behaviors with their children, not because of a conscious choice but because it is the only parenting model they know.

It is essential to recognize that attachment styles are not static and can change over time with self-awareness and effort. Parents who identify with an insecure attachment style can seek therapy and support to develop healthier ways of relating to their children. By doing so, they can break the cycle of emotional immaturity and foster a more secure and nurturing environment for their family.

As we move forward, it is crucial to consider the psychological underpinnings of emotional immaturity and the broader societal and cultural contexts that shape parenting practices. These external influences can either exacerbate the challenges faced by emotionally immature parents or provide avenues for support and growth.

Societal and Cultural Influences

In exploring the origins of emotional immaturity in parents, it is essential to consider the broader societal and cultural influences that shape individual behaviors and attitudes. While the attachment styles discussed earlier play a significant role in the development of emotional maturity, the environment in which a person is raised and continues to live can exert a powerful influence on their emotional development.

Society and culture are invisible forces dictating norms, values, and expectations. These forces can either support emotional growth or stifle it. In many cultures, there is an emphasis on maintaining social harmony and overexpressing individual emotions, which can lead to adults who are adept at keeping the peace but need to be more skilled at recognizing and managing their feelings or those of their children. This can result in a form of emotional neglect, where parents may provide for the physical needs of their children but remain disconnected from their emotional needs.

Furthermore, certain cultural narratives glorify self-sacrifice and the suppression of personal needs for the sake of family or community. Parents who internalize these values may struggle to model healthy emotional boundaries for their children. They might prioritize the external appearance of a well-functioning family while neglecting the emotional dialogues that foster intimacy and understanding.

In addition to cultural narratives, societal structures and pressures contribute to emotional immaturity. The relentless pace of modern life, the emphasis on material success, and the often unattainable standards of perfection can leave parents feeling inadequate and overwhelmed. This chronic stress can impede their ability to be present and emotionally responsive to their children. When parents are preoccupied with the demands of work and the pursuit of status, they may inadvertently model a disconnection from their inner emotional world.

Moreover, the rise of digital technology and social media has created a new landscape for parental emotional immaturity. The constant bombardment of curated images of 'perfect' families and parenting can create unrealistic expectations and a sense of failure. Parents may focus more on projecting an ideal image than engaging in the messy, authentic emotional exchanges that genuine relationships require.

It is also essential to recognize the intergenerational transmission of emotional patterns. Parents who are emotionally immature caregivers may not have had the opportunity to learn healthy emotional regulation and expression. Without conscious effort and support, these patterns can be passed down, perpetuating a cycle of emotional disconnect.

Understanding the societal and cultural influences on emotional immaturity is not about assigning blame but gaining insight into the complex web of factors contributing to this issue. By recognizing these influences, parents and those who support them can begin to identify the changes needed to foster emotional growth and maturity, both for themselves and for the next generation.

As we move forward, it becomes clear that while societal and cultural influences are significant, they are not the only factors at play. Individual experiences, particularly those involving trauma, can have a profound impact on emotional development. Addressing these personal histories is crucial in breaking the cycle of emotional immaturity.

Trauma and Its Aftermath

Trauma can be a chisel that shapes the psyche in profound and often unsettling ways. When considering the development of emotional immaturity in parents, it is essential to explore the role that traumatic experiences may play in this dynamic. Trauma, particularly when experienced during one's formative years, can arrest emotional development, leading to behaviors and patterns that persist into adulthood and parenthood.

In the wake of trauma, individuals often adopt coping mechanisms that can be maladaptive. While initially serving as a means of psychological survival, these mechanisms can become entrenched and manifest as emotional immaturity. For instance, a parent who experienced abandonment as a child might struggle with emotional availability, fearing that closeness will inevitably lead to loss. Alternatively, a parent who endured emotional abuse may find it challenging to engage in healthy communication, perhaps resorting to sarcasm or withdrawal in times of stress.

The aftermath of trauma can also lead to a preoccupation with control, as unpredictability may feel intolerable to someone whose past was marked by chaotic or harmful experiences. This need for control can stifle the spontaneity and openness required for nurturing parent-child relationships. It can also lead to rigidity in thinking and behavior, making it difficult for such parents to adapt to the evolving needs of their children or to model emotional resilience.

Moreover, trauma can impair a person's ability to self-regulate emotions. Parents who have not had the opportunity or support to process their traumatic experiences may be prone to emotional outbursts or, conversely, emotional numbness. Both extremes create an environment where children may struggle to learn healthy emotional regulation themselves.

It is essential to recognize that trauma does not destine one to become an emotionally immature parent. Many individuals demonstrate remarkable resilience and, with support and healing, can break the cycle of trauma to become emotionally attuned caregivers. However, without addressing the wounds of the past, the likelihood of perpetuating patterns of emotional immaturity increases.

Compassion is a critical component in addressing the intergenerational impact of trauma. By understanding the origins of a parent's emotional struggles, families can begin to foster an environment of healing and growth. This often involves professional support, such as therapy, which can provide the tools and space for individuals to work through their traumatic experiences and develop healthier emotional habits.

In this context, it is crucial to approach the subject of emotionally immature parents not with judgment but with an empathetic understanding of the complex interplay between past trauma and present behavior. By doing so, we can open pathways to healing and transformation that benefit the parents and their children and the familial legacy they will leave behind.

Chapter Summary

- Emotional immaturity in parents often stems from generational patterns and unresolved psychological conflicts.
- Children learn emotional responses from their parents, which can affect their emotional development if they are immature.

- Cultural norms and societal expectations can reinforce emotional immaturity by discouraging emotional expression.
- Historical traumas experienced by families can lead to emotional scars that affect future generations.
- Psychological theories like Freud's psychoanalytic theory and Erikson's stages of development help explain emotional immaturity.
- Attachment styles formed in childhood influence how parents relate to their children and can perpetuate emotional immaturity.
- Societal pressures and cultural narratives can contribute to emotional immaturity by emphasizing material success over emotional connection.
- Trauma, especially in early life, can arrest emotional development and lead to maladaptive coping mechanisms in parents.

2

PROFILES OF EMOTIONALLY IMMATURE PARENTS

The Narcissistic Parent

In the landscape of emotionally immature parenting, the narcissistic parent often casts a long shadow, one that can shape the emotional terrain of a child's life in profound ways. An overarching self-interest and a deep need for admiration and validation characterize this type of parent. Their emotional immaturity is not marked by a lack of intelligence or love but rather by a self-centered approach to relationships that can leave their children feeling secondary to their parent's desires and image.

The narcissistic parent may present a polished and charming façade to the outside world, often appearing confident and accomplished. To their children, however, they can be unpredictable and sometimes cruel, as their need for control and adoration takes precedence over the child's needs for support and autonomy. It is not uncommon for these parents to have high expectations of their children, not necessarily for the child's benefit, but as a reflection of their image. Children may feel pressured to perform or conform to their parent's idealized vision, leading to a sense of inadequacy and a lack of genuine self-esteem.

One of the hallmarks of the narcissistic parent is their inability to empathize with their child. They struggle to recognize and respond to their child's feelings as separate from their own. When a child expresses needs or emotions that do not align with the parent's self-image or agenda, the parent may react with indifference, irritation, or hostility. This lack of attunement can lead to a child doubting their feelings and experiences, often carrying into adulthood a tendency to dismiss their emotional needs.

The relationship dynamics with a narcissistic parent can be particularly challenging because the parent may use affection and approval as tools for manipulation. Love and attention may be given conditionally, withdrawn as a form of punishment, or used to coax the child into compliance. This inconsistency can create an anxious attachment in the child, who learns to be hyper-vigilant to the parent's moods and prioritize their emotional state over their own.

Despite these challenges, it is essential to recognize that the child of a narcissistic parent can learn to navigate this complex relationship and develop a strong sense of self. With support, understanding, and perhaps therapeutic intervention, individuals can work through the confusion and hurt that may come from being raised by a narcissistic parent. They can learn to set boundaries, cultivate self-compassion, and build healthy relationships that affirm their worth and autonomy.

As we continue to explore the profiles of emotionally immature parents, it becomes clear that each type presents unique challenges and opportunities for growth. Understanding these profiles helps us empathize with those who have been shaped by such relationships and empowers us to break cycles of emotional immaturity for future generations.

The Authoritarian Parent

The authoritarian parent stands as a figure of unwavering control and rigid expectations. Unlike the narcissistic parent, whose self-absorption can lead to a volatile and unpredictable environment, the authoritarian parent creates a world with clearly defined rules and roles, leaving little room for flexibility or open dialogue.

The authoritarian parent's approach to child-rearing is characterized by a strict adherence to discipline and a focus on obedience. They often believe that children should be seen and not heard and that questioning parental authority is tantamount to disrespect. This type of parent values order and tradition, and they often rely on the phrase "because I said so" as a final word to shut down any form of negotiation or protest.

Children raised by authoritarian parents may learn to follow the rules well. Still, they often do so at the expense of their self-expression and autonomy. The fear of punishment or disapproval can lead these children to become excellent rule-followers. Still, they may struggle with self-esteem and the ability to think independently. They may also associate love and acceptance with performance and compliance, which can carry into their adult relationships and self-perception.

The emotional immaturity of the authoritarian parent is evident in their inability to empathize with their children's feelings and needs. They focus on maintaining control rather than fostering an environment where children can safely express emotions and learn through trial and error. This can result in a disconnect between parent and child, where the child feels that their emotional world is neither understood nor valued.

It is essential to recognize that the authoritarian parent's behavior often stems from their upbringing or a deep-seated fear of chaos and disorder. They may equate control with care and believe that by enforcing strict rules, they are preparing their children for the world's harsh realities. However, this can inadvertently stifle a child's development of critical life skills such as problem-solving, negotiation, and emotional regulation.

In contrast to the authoritarian parent's rigidity, other parenting styles offer a more balanced approach, where structure is present but not suffocating and where children are encouraged to develop a sense of self within safe boundaries. As we continue to explore the various profiles of emotionally immature parents, it becomes increasingly clear that the emotional health of a parent plays a pivotal role in the emotional development of their children. The key lies in finding a balance that nurtures discipline and dialogue, allowing children to grow into emotionally mature and resilient adults.

The Permissive Parent

The permissive parent often stands in stark contrast to the authoritarian figure we have previously explored. Where the authoritarian imposes rigid boundaries and high expectations, the permissive parent is characterized by a notable lack of them. This type of parent may appear more as a friend than a guardian, often driven by an aversion to conflict and a deep-seated desire to be liked by their children.

An indulgent attitude typically marks the permissive parent's approach. They may allow their children to set their schedules, make their own decisions, and face few consequences for misbehavior. This laissez-faire style is not born of a lack of love or concern; rather, it often stems from the parent's own emotional needs and insecurities. They may feel incapable of setting and enforcing rules or fear that by doing so, they will push their children away.

While this might create a household with a seemingly relaxed atmosphere, the long-term effects on children can be profound. With clear boundaries and consistent guidance, children may be able to develop self-discipline and an understanding of appropriate behavior. They may also form an unrealistic view of the world, one in which their actions do not have significant consequences, which can lead to challenges in their adult lives, particularly in professional environments or personal relationships where structure and accountability are essential.

The permissive parent's emotional immaturity is often reflected in their inability to tolerate the everyday stresses of parenting. They may seek to avoid the discomfort of being the 'bad guy' and thus shirk the responsibility of disciplining their children. This avoidance can be deeply rooted in their own experiences of being parented, perhaps mirroring the permissive or neglectful styles they were subjected to.

Children of permissive parents may also find themselves feeling a sense of emptiness or lack of direction. While they may not have experienced the overt control of an authoritarian parent, they lack the secure framework to test their limits and learn from their mistakes. As these children grow, they may seek out or create structure in other areas of their lives to compensate for what was missing in their upbringing.

It is essential to recognize that permissive parenting, like other styles, is often an unconscious replication of the parent's emotional world. Compassion for the parent and the child is crucial in understanding this dynamic. The permissive parent is not without love or good intentions; they are often unequipped to provide the structure and consistent guidance that is a cornerstone of mature parenting.

As we move forward in our exploration of emotionally immature parents, we will encounter the enmeshed parent whose intense involvement in their child's life presents a different set of challenges and impacts on the child's development. Understanding the nuances of each parenting style allows us to see the spectrum of emotional immaturity and its diverse manifestations within family dynamics.

The Enmeshed Parent

The enmeshed parent presents a unique set of challenges and characteristics that can profoundly affect the family dynamic. Unlike the permissive parent, who may take a more hands-off approach, the enmeshed parent is excessively involved and often oversteps personal boundaries, leading to an intricately intertwined relationship with their child to the point where individual identities seem blurred.

The enmeshed parent often sees no distinction between their emotional needs and their child's. They may rely on their child for support, companionship, and even emotional stability, placing an undue burden on the child's shoulders. This can manifest in various ways, from the parent sharing inappropriate personal details and treating the child as a confidant to expecting the child to fulfill emotional roles typically reserved for an adult partner.

This dynamic can lead to several developmental issues for the child. As they grow, these children may struggle with forming a sense of self, as their needs and emotions have been deeply entangled with their parents. They may have difficulty recognizing where their parent's feelings end and begin, which can lead to challenges in establishing healthy relationships outside the family unit.

The enmeshed parent's inability to recognize and respect boundaries often stems from their emotional immaturity. They may have an intense fear of abandonment or loneliness, which drives them to cling to their child. This can create a suffocating environment for the child, who may feel responsible for the parent's emotional well-being in the absence of appropriate boundaries.

Children of enmeshed parents may also exhibit high loyalty and devotion to their parents, often at the expense of their own needs and desires. This loyalty is not born out of a healthy, reciprocal relationship but out of a sense of obligation and the fear of what might happen if they do not meet their parent's emotional demands.

As these children transition into adulthood, they may encounter a host of issues, such as codependency in relationships, difficulty with decision-making, and a pervasive sense of guilt when asserting independence. While often rooted in the parent's deep love for their child, the enmeshed relationship can inadvertently stifle the child's growth into a fully autonomous individual.

It is crucial for those who have grown up with an enmeshed parent to recognize that their intense entanglement is not the blueprint for all relationships. Healing and growth come with understanding the dynamics of enmeshment and learning to establish healthy boundaries. This process often involves redefining one's sense of self apart from the parent and engaging in self-exploration and personal development.

For parents who identify with enmeshment tendencies, it is equally important to seek help understanding the origins of their behaviors and to learn how to foster a supportive yet independent relationship with their children. Through this, they can encourage their children's individuality and autonomy, essential for their emotional and psychological well-being.

In the broader context of emotionally immature parenting, the enmeshed parent represents a pattern where love and care, though undoubtedly present, are expressed in ways that can hinder rather than nurture. Through compassionate self-awareness and a commitment to change, parents and children can navigate the complexities of enmeshment and move towards healthier, more fulfilling relationships.

The Absent Parent

In the landscape of familial relationships, the figure of the absent parent is a stark contrast to the enmeshed parent we discussed earlier. Emotionally immature parents can manifest in various forms, and the absent parent is characterized by a pervasive detachment from their child's emotional world. This detachment is not necessarily physical; an absent parent can be present in the home but emotionally distant, creating an environment where a child may feel alone even in the company of family.

The absent parent often seems preoccupied with their own needs and interests, which can overshadow their child's emotional and sometimes even physical needs. This type of parent may avoid involvement in their child's life, not out of a lack of love but because they are overwhelmed by the demands of parenting or are simply ill-equipped to handle the emotional complexities of it. They may be seen as aloof or indifferent, and their interactions with their child can feel perfunctory or superficial.

Children of absent parents may struggle with feelings of abandonment. They may question their self-worth, wondering why they do not seem to merit their parent's attention or care. They might become excessively self-reliant, learning early on that they cannot depend on their parent for emotional support. This self-reliance can be a double-edged sword, fostering independence while reinforcing a deep-seated belief that they must go through life's challenges alone.

The emotional void left by an absent parent can lead to significant developmental impacts. A child may grow up with a skewed perception of relationships, believing emotional disconnection is typical. They may also need help recognizing or expressing their emotions, having never been taught or shown how to do so healthily.

Acknowledging that the absent parent is not always absent by choice is essential. Factors such as mental health issues, substance abuse, or a history of being raised by emotionally immature parents themselves can contribute to their detachment. Compassion for both the parent and child is crucial in understanding this dynamic. Healing can begin with recognizing the absent parent's limitations and the child's unmet emotional needs.

As we navigate through the complexities of emotionally immature parents, it becomes evident that the patterns established in childhood can profoundly influence one's emotional landscape into adulthood. The journey toward understanding and healing is a complex path. Still, with insight and support, individuals can learn to fill the gaps an absent parent leaves and build fulfilling emotional connections in their lives.

Chapter Summary

- The narcissistic parent prioritizes their own needs for admiration and control, often at the expense of their child's emotional well-being.
- Children of narcissistic parents may feel pressured to meet their parent's expectations and struggle with self-esteem and empathy.
- The authoritarian parent enforces strict discipline and obedience, often stifling a child's autonomy and self-expression.
- Children raised by authoritarian parents may become rule-followers with issues in self-esteem and independent thinking.
- The permissive parent avoids conflict and sets few boundaries, leading to children who may lack self-discipline and understanding of consequences.
- The enmeshed parent overly involves themselves in their child's life, blurring boundaries and hindering the child's development of a separate identity.
- The absent parent is emotionally detached, leaving children feeling abandoned and questioning their self-worth.
- Each emotionally immature parent presents unique challenges. Still, individuals can navigate these relationships and foster personal growth with support and understanding.

3

THE CHILD'S PERSPECTIVE

Growing Up with Emotional Neglect

In the tender landscape of childhood, where the soil of self is still being tilled, the presence of emotionally immature parents can cast long shadows over the growth of a young psyche. Emotional neglect, a silent arbiter of pain, often goes unnoticed by the world outside the family unit. Yet, its impact is deeply felt by those who endure it.

For children in such environments, the absence of emotional attunement from their caregivers can be as stark as the absence of food or warmth. These children may learn to walk on tiptoe around the moods and whims of their parents, internalizing a belief that their feelings are secondary or, worse, irrelevant. The lack of validation for their emotional experiences can lead to a profound sense of loneliness and a belief that they are inherently flawed.

Emotional neglect from an immature parent often means that the child's emotional needs are not met with consistency or understanding. A parent may be physically present but emotionally distant, unable to engage with the child's inner world. The child learns to mute their emotional responses and to become self-reliant in their inner emotional landscape because the external support is unpredictable or nonexistent.

While a testament to the child's resilience, this self-reliance comes at a cost. The child may grow up feeling disconnected from their emotions, struggling to identify and express them. They may become adept at reading the emotional cues of others yet find themselves at a loss when it comes to interpreting their feelings. The need for validation, for someone to acknowledge and affirm their emotional reality, can become a silent yearning. This quest shapes their interactions and relationships into adulthood.

As these children navigate the complexities of life, they often carry with them the weight of unvalidated emotions. The quest for validation is not merely a search for affirmation from others but a more profound journey towards self-acknowledgment and self-compassion. It is about learning to recognize the validity of one's emotions and experiences despite the lack of recognition from their primary caregivers.

The journey towards healing and self-validation is arduous but manageable. It involves peeling back the layers of self-protection, unlearning the patterns of emotional neglect, and building a relationship with oneself that is based on kindness, acceptance, and understanding. It is about finding one's voice and learning to trust that voice as a guide towards a more integrated and emotionally fulfilling life.

In the next steps of this journey, we will explore the paths individuals take in their quest for validation, understanding how they seek to fill the void left by their upbringing and how they can ultimately find the validation they need.

The Quest for Validation

In a child's heart, the yearning for a parent's approval and understanding is as natural as breathing. Children often embark on a silent, solitary quest for validation when the guardians of their world are emotionally immature. This quest can shape their identities and color their perceptions of self-worth for years.

For these children, validation is not merely a want; it is an unmet need, a puzzle piece missing from their emotional development. It is the acknowledgment they crave that their feelings are real, their experiences are legitimate, and their existence is significant. In the absence of this recognition from emotionally immature parents, children may question the validity of their emotions and experiences, leading to a deep-seated sense of invisibility.

The quest for validation in the eyes of a child living with emotional neglect is a journey fraught with confusion. They may wonder why their accomplishments, however grand or small, often go unnoticed or are met with indifference. They may internalize the lack of emotional response as a reflection of their worth, mistakenly believing they do not deserve attention or praise.

As they grow, these children may become adept at reading their parents' subtle cues and moods, adjusting their behavior in the hope of eliciting a positive response. They may become performers in their lives, playing roles they believe will garner the validation they deeply desire. Yet, the applause they seek is often absent, and the curtain falls on their efforts without the anticipated acclaim.

The emotional toll of this quest can manifest in various ways. Some children may become overachievers, relentlessly pushing themselves in academics, sports, or other activities as they chase the elusive approval of their parents. Others may withdraw, becoming quiet observers in their homes, convinced that their voices are not worthy of being heard.

Despite these challenges, the quest for validation is also a testament to the resilience of the human spirit. While marked by heartache, it is a journey that can lead to a profound understanding of self-reliance and inner strength. These children may learn to seek validation from within, to trust their own emotions and judgments, and to build a sense of self-worth that is not contingent on the unpredictable responses of emotionally immature parents.

As we delve deeper into the experiences of these children, we will explore the coping mechanisms and survival strategies they develop in response to their complex emotional environments. While necessary for navigating childhood, these adaptations can impact their adult lives, influencing their relationships, self-image, and how they parent their children.

In understanding the quest for validation, we open a window into the hearts of those who have navigated the turbulent waters of emotional neglect. Through this empathetic lens, we can begin to appreciate the full scope of their resilience and the depth of their desire to be seen, heard, and valued.

Coping Mechanisms and Survival Strategies

For many, the presence of emotionally immature parents can cast long shadows over the growth of a young psyche. In their innate resilience and adaptability, children often develop a repertoire of coping mechanisms and survival strategies to navigate the unpredictable terrain of their caregivers' emotional volatility.

One such coping mechanism is adopting a role that provides a sense of stability within the family dynamic. The child may become the 'caretaker,' shouldering responsibilities far beyond their years, or the 'peacemaker,' constantly diffusing tensions to maintain harmony. While offering a temporary haven of predictability, these roles can also stifle the child's authentic development, as they contort themselves into shapes that please their parents rather than explore their identities.

Another common strategy is emotional camouflage. Children learn to mask their true feelings, presenting a façade that aligns with their parents' expectations. This can manifest as a perpetual agreeableness, a suppression of negative emotions, or an exaggerated display of traits that garner approval. The cost of this masquerade is often a deep sense of loneliness and a disconnection from their emotional core.

Some children find solace in the world of imagination, creating rich inner lives that offer refuge from the emotional barrenness of their surroundings. This inner sanctuary can foster creativity and resilience. Still, it may also lead to a sense of alienation from the external world, as the child retreats further into their mental haven to escape the emotional neglect or unpredictability they face.

Intellectualization is another fortress to which a child might retreat. The child creates a buffer against the emotional chaos at home by focusing on logic, facts, and learning. This pursuit of knowledge can be empowering, but it may also serve as a barrier against the vulnerability of emotional connection, leaving the child adept at reasoning but hesitant in matters of the heart.

In some cases, children become hyper-vigilant, attuned to the slightest shifts in their parents' moods or behaviors. This heightened alertness can be protective, allowing the child to anticipate and navigate potential conflicts. However, it can also lead to chronic anxiety and an inability to relax, as the child remains perpetually on guard for the next emotional upheaval.

It is essential to recognize that these coping mechanisms and survival strategies, while adaptive in a challenging home environment, can have long-term implications. As these children grow into adulthood, they may find that the very behaviors that once protected them now hinder their ability to form healthy relationships, pursue their true passions, or allow themselves to be vulnerable and authentic.

The journey of healing and growth for those who have navigated childhood with emotionally immature parents involves a delicate unraveling of these ingrained patterns. It requires a compassionate self-exploration and the courage to face the pain that was once too overwhelming for a child to bear. It is a path of reclaiming oneself, piece by piece and learning to thrive beyond survival.

The Sibling Experience

Growing up with emotionally immature parents can be a solitary journey. Still, when siblings are part of the family dynamic, the experience takes on additional complexity. Siblings may become allies, adversaries, or strangers to one another, depending on how they navigate the unpredictable emotional landscape set by their parents.

In some cases, siblings bond over their shared challenges. They find solace in knowing someone else truly understands their parents' erratic moods and demands. These siblings often develop a secret language of glances and gestures, a silent communication that speaks volumes of their mutual support. They may protect each other from emotional outbursts and even take on parental roles, providing the care and guidance they are not receiving.

However, the strain of an emotionally volatile household can also drive siblings apart. Competition for the limited resources of parental attention and affection can foster resentment. An emotionally immature parent may, intentionally or not, set siblings against each other, comparing them or using one to control the other. This can lead to a dynamic where siblings feel pitted against one another, each struggling to carve out their own space and identity within the family.

In families where one child is designated as the "golden child" and another as the "scapegoat," the disparity in treatment can create deep rifts. The favored child may feel guilty for the special treatment they receive, or they may internalize the belief that they are more deserving. Conversely, the scapegoated child may harbor feelings of unworthiness and resentment. These roles can become entrenched, following the siblings into adulthood and affecting their relationships for years.

Sometimes, a sibling may take on the role of the caretaker or "parentified" child, especially if they are significantly older than their siblings. This responsibility can be a heavy burden, as they sacrifice their needs and childhood to provide stability and support. The parentified child may struggle with resentment and loss, even as they love their siblings deeply and feel proud of their ability to care for them.

The emotional neglect and inconsistency often accompanying immature parenting can also lead siblings to disengage. They may grow up feeling like strangers, each retreating into their worlds as a means of self-preservation. Without the tools or examples to build healthy relationships, they may find it challenging to connect in meaningful ways, even as they long for a deeper bond.

As these siblings mature and reflect on their upbringing, they may grapple with complex emotions. The shared history of navigating their parents' emotional immaturity can be both a source of connection and a barrier to it. Some may find that they can reach out to their siblings with greater understanding and compassion as they heal, forging new relationships built on mutual respect and shared growth.

Others may find that the gap needs to be narrower or the behavior patterns too profoundly ingrained to bridge the divide. In these instances, the journey may be individual healing, learning to find peace with the past, and building a sense of family and community in other areas of their lives.

The sibling experience in the context of emotionally immature parents is as varied as the individuals involved. Each sibling navigates the terrain with their map, shaped by their unique perceptions and responses to their family environment. The paths they take can lead to incredibly resilient bonds or to painfully deep divides. Understanding these dynamics is crucial for anyone seeking to heal from such a childhood and those seeking to support them.

Adulthood Reckonings

As we journey through the landscape of adulthood, the long shadows cast by emotionally immature parents often stretch far beyond the confines of childhood. For many, realizing a parent's emotional immaturity crystallizes not in the throes of adolescence but in the fullness of adult life. This reckoning, while deeply personal, is a shared experience among those who have navigated the unpredictable waters of a childhood overshadowed by a parent's emotional limitations.

In this stage of life, the child-now-adult begins to piece together the mosaic of their upbringing, often with the clarity that distance and independence afford. It is a time when the fog of confusion lifts, and the patterns of emotional immaturity that characterized their parents' behavior become starkly apparent. The once inexplicable reactions, the absence of empathy, or the relentless self-centeredness of a parent are now understood as part and parcel of a broader, more troubling dynamic.

This dawning of understanding, however, is not without its pain. There is a profound sense of grief that accompanies the recognition of what was missed in one's formative years—a nurturing stability, a sense of security, or the unconditional support that every child deserves. The adult child might grapple with a sense of loss for the emotional connection that was never fully realized, and perhaps, a mourning for the parent they needed but did not have.

Yet, within this reckoning lies the growth potential. It is an opportunity to break the cycle of emotional immaturity. The adult child, through reflection and often with the support of therapy or self-help resources, can begin to cultivate the emotional skills they were not taught. They learn to set boundaries, articulate their needs, and seek out reciprocal and nurturing relationships. This process is not linear; it is fraught with the challenges of unlearning deeply ingrained behaviors and the temptation to fall back into familiar patterns.

For some, this period also prompts a reevaluation of the relationship with their emotionally immature parents. Decisions must be made about the nature of that relationship moving forward. Can there be a dialogue, an understanding, or is the distance necessary for self-preservation? These are not choices made lightly but require a compassionate yet firm resolve.

In navigating these waters, the adult child may also find solace and solidarity with their siblings, as discussed previously. The shared history can be a source of mutual support. Still, it can also reveal divergent paths of coping and understanding. Each sibling's journey is unique, and how they reconcile their childhood experiences with their adult lives can vary widely.

The reckoning of adulthood is a testament to the resilience of the human spirit. It is about reclaiming one's narrative and stepping into an identity not defined by a parent's emotional shortcomings. It is about learning to parent oneself to provide the love, patience, and encouragement everyone deserves. And in this journey, there is hope—not only for the individual but for the generations that follow, as the cycle of emotional immaturity is acknowledged, understood, and, with determination and heart, finally broken.

Chapter Summary

- Emotional neglect by immature parents can profoundly affect a child's development, leading to feelings of loneliness and a belief in their inherent flaws.
- Children with emotionally distant parents learn to suppress their emotions and become self-reliant, which can disconnect them from their feelings and hinder emotional expression.
- The quest for validation becomes a central theme in these children's lives as they seek acknowledgment of their emotional experiences from others and, ultimately, themselves.
- Coping mechanisms developed in childhood, such as adopting specific roles or emotional camouflage, can long-term affect adult relationships and self-image.
- Siblings in such families may become allies or adversaries, with their relationships affected by the competition for parental attention or by taking on parental roles themselves.
- In adulthood, individuals with emotionally immature parents often experience a reckoning as they gain clarity on their upbringing and work to break the cycle of emotional immaturity.

- Adult children may need to reevaluate their relationship with their parents, setting boundaries or seeking distance for self-preservation.
- The journey towards healing involves self-compassion, learning to validate one's emotions, and building healthier relationships and self-identity.

4

COMMUNICATION BREAKDOWNS AND BARRIERS

The Language of Emotional Immaturity

In navigating the complex dynamics of families with emotionally immature parents, we often encounter a peculiar dialect—a language of emotional immaturity that can perplex and frustrate those who yearn for genuine connection and understanding. This language, marked by its own set of rules and patterns, can create significant communication barriers between parents and children, and it is essential to recognize its features to foster better relationships and healing.

Emotionally immature parents may communicate indirectly, favoring hints and suggestions over clear and direct expression. This can leave their children in constant guesswork, trying to decipher the underlying messages or expectations. Such indirectness can stem from a parent's discomfort with vulnerability, fear of confrontation, or lack of awareness about effectively communicating.

Another characteristic of this language is minimization or trivialization, especially when faced with their child's emotions or needs. A parent might respond to a child's sadness or anger with comments like "Don't be so sensitive" or "It's not a big deal." This dismissive approach invalidates the child's experience and teaches them to doubt their own feelings and suppress their emotional expression.

Moreover, emotionally immature parents might resort to blame-shifting as a defense mechanism. When confronted with a mistake or a situation that requires accountability, they might deflect responsibility onto others, including their children. This can manifest in statements that imply the child is the cause of the parent's negative emotions or that the child's behavior is the sole problem, overlooking the parent's role in the dynamic.

Projection is another standard linguistic tool in the repertoire of emotionally immature communication. Parents may project their feelings, desires, or insecurities onto their children, accusing them of having motives or emotions that reflect the parent's internal world. This can be confusing and damaging to a child's sense of self as they struggle to separate their own identity from the distorted mirror their parent holds up to them.

Lastly, emotional immaturity can lead to a lack of consistency in communication. Parents may swing from being overly involved and controlling to being distant and disengaged, leaving their children unsure of where they stand. This inconsistency can create an unstable emotional environment where children must walk on eggshells, wondering which version of their parent they will encounter.

Understanding the language of emotional immaturity is crucial in breaking down the communication barriers in families with such dynamics. By recognizing these patterns, children of emotionally immature parents can begin to find their voice, establish boundaries, and seek healthier ways of relating both within and outside their family system. It is a journey that requires patience, self-compassion, and, often, the support of others who can provide the perspective and validation that emotionally immature parents may be unable to offer.

Avoidance and Denial

In the realm of family dynamics, the presence of emotionally immature parents can lead to a unique set of communication challenges. One of the most pervasive is the tendency toward avoidance and denial. This behavior can create an environment where open dialogue is stifled and emotional honesty is scarce.

In this context, avoidance manifests as an unwillingness to engage in conversations that might lead to emotional discomfort or require self-reflection. Emotionally immature parents may skillfully change the subject, make light of serious topics, or even physically remove themselves from situations that demand a more profound emotional engagement. This evasion is often not malicious but rather a profoundly ingrained defense mechanism. It is a way of preserving a self-image that may feel threatened by the vulnerability of such discussions.

On the other hand, denial is a more direct refusal to acknowledge the reality of a situation or the validity of another's feelings. When children, even adult children, attempt to express how certain behaviors have impacted them, emotionally immature parents may outright deny any wrongdoing or the emotional fallout of their actions. This denial can be particularly damaging as it invalidates the child's experiences and feelings, often leading to a sense of confusion and emotional isolation.

The interplay between avoidance and denial creates a barrier to authentic connection. Children of such parents may find themselves perpetually on the outskirts of genuine emotional intimacy, unable to penetrate the armor of avoidance and denial. This dynamic can leave children feeling unseen and unheard, with a gnawing sense that their emotional reality is neither acknowledged nor valued.

Understanding this pattern is crucial for those who find themselves in the shadow of emotionally immature parents. Recognizing avoidance and denial for what they are—defensive strategies rather than reflections of one's worth—can be the first step toward healing. It is also important to note that these behaviors are often deeply rooted in the parents' unresolved emotional issues, which they may be unconscious of or unwilling to confront.

For those navigating these waters, seeking out supportive relationships and environments where open and honest communication is possible and encouraged is essential. Establishing boundaries with parents who exhibit these behaviors can be challenging but is often necessary to protect one's emotional well-being.

In the journey toward understanding and healing, it is helpful to approach these situations with compassion—for oneself and, if possible, for the emotionally immature parents. Compassion does not mean accepting hurtful behaviors but rather acknowledging the complex emotional landscape that every individual navigates, often with imperfect tools.

As we move forward, it is essential to consider how the avoidance and denial of emotionally immature parents can escalate into patterns of conflict and criticism, further complicating the family dynamic. By addressing these issues with empathy and insight, we can dismantle the communication barriers and foster a more nurturing and emotionally mature environment.

Conflict and Criticism

In navigating relationships with emotionally immature parents, we often find ourselves entrenched in patterns of conflict and criticism that can feel both bewildering and disheartening. This dynamic is a source of pain and a significant barrier to healthy communication.

When emotionally immature parents face conflict, their responses can be unpredictable and frequently disproportionate to the situation. Instead of approaching disagreements with a willingness to understand and resolve, these parents may react defensively, perceiving any form of dissent as a personal attack. This defensiveness can manifest as a barrage of criticism, often leaving their children devalued and misunderstood.

Criticism from a parent, especially when it is constant and harsh, can profoundly impact a child's self-esteem. It can create an environment where the child feels perpetually on trial, always preparing a defense for their actions and choices. This relentless scrutiny can foster a sense of walking on eggshells, where open and honest communication is replaced by a strategy of avoidance or placation to prevent further criticism.

Moreover, emotionally immature parents may lack the self-awareness to recognize the effects of their critical behavior. They might justify their actions as a form of 'tough love' or necessary guidance, not realizing the emotional toll it takes on their children. This lack of insight into their behavior and its repercussions can make it difficult for their children to broach the subject without inciting further conflict.

In these circumstances, children may adopt roles that do not align with their true selves merely to appease their parents and avoid confrontation. This can lead to a suppression of their own needs and desires, which, over time, can result in a loss of personal identity and agency.

The challenge, then, is to navigate this minefield of criticism to preserve one's sense of self while attempting to maintain a relationship with the parent. It requires a delicate balance of asserting one's needs and perspectives without exacerbating the cycle of conflict and criticism.

To move forward, developing strategies for self-protection and self-care becomes essential, including setting boundaries, seeking support from others, and finding constructive ways to express one's needs and desires. It is a journey that involves recognizing the limitations of the parent's emotional capacity while also honoring one's emotional well-being.

In the subsequent exploration of our journey, we will delve into the intricacies of expressing needs and desires in the shadow of emotionally immature parents, seeking pathways to authentic communication and self-expression.

Expressing Needs and Desires

In the realm of family dynamics, mainly when dealing with emotionally immature parents, the ability to effectively express needs and desires often becomes a convoluted endeavor. The communication barriers that arise in such relationships can be both subtle and profound, influencing the immediate interactions and the long-term emotional well-being of the children involved.

When a child attempts to convey their needs to an emotionally immature parent, they may encounter a range of dismissive responses. These parents might respond with indifference, irritation, or even mockery, which sends a clear message to the child that their needs are not of paramount importance. Over time, this invalidation pattern can lead to a deep sense of being misunderstood and neglected.

The challenge here is multifaceted. On the one hand, children of emotionally immature parents often learn to suppress their desires, adapting to the emotional landscape by becoming excessively self-reliant or by mirroring the emotional detachment of their caregivers. On the other hand, these children might also engage in heightened emotional displays, hoping that their increased efforts will finally break through the barriers and elicit the desired response from their parents.

However, such strategies rarely yield the connection and understanding they seek. Emotionally immature parents, by nature, struggle with empathy and are often preoccupied with their own emotional experiences. This self-focus can make it difficult for them to recognize and respond to the emotional cues of others, including their children. Consequently, children may feel that their emotional needs are unmet and entirely unseen.

To navigate this complex terrain, it is essential for children, and later as adults, to develop a keen awareness of their own emotional needs and to cultivate the skills necessary to articulate them. This often requires external support, such as therapy or guidance from emotionally mature mentors, to learn how to express themselves in a manner that is both clear and self-affirming.

Moreover, finding alternative sources of emotional support outside the family unit can be crucial. Establishing relationships with friends, partners, or community members who demonstrate emotional maturity can provide a contrasting experience where the expression of needs and desires is not only accepted but encouraged.

In seeking these healthier dynamics, individuals learn that their emotional needs are valid and that expressing them is not only permissible but necessary for their psychological health. They also understand that while they may not be able to change the emotional immaturity of their parents, they can change how they interact with them and set boundaries to protect their well-being.

Ultimately, the journey of expressing needs and desires in the context of emotionally immature parents is one of self-discovery and empowerment. It is about finding one's voice amid silence and learning to speak one's truth, even when it might not be heard by those we most crave acknowledgment. It is a testament to the resilience of the human spirit and the enduring quest for emotional connection and understanding.

The Struggle for Autonomy

When dealing with emotionally immature parents, children often find themselves in a silent tug-of-war for autonomy. This struggle is not marked by overt confrontations but by subtle yet profound undercurrents of control and resistance. Autonomy – the right to self-governance and independence – becomes a battleground where communication often falters, and barriers are erected, sometimes unwittingly.

For the child of an emotionally immature parent, the quest for autonomy can feel like an uphill battle. The parent may often unconsciously perceive the child's growing independence as a threat to their sense of control or self-worth. They might employ tactics that undermine the child's confidence and decision-making abilities. This can manifest in various ways, such as dismissing the child's opinions, overruling their choices, or using guilt to manipulate them into compliance.

The child's natural desire for parental approval and love further complicates the struggle for autonomy. This desire can create a conflict within the child, torn between asserting their individuality and preserving the emotional bond with their parent. The child may self-censor, suppress their true desires, or second-guess their instincts to maintain peace or avoid the emotional fallout that often accompanies attempts at self-assertion.

Moreover, the child may internalize the belief that their value is contingent upon meeting their parent's expectations or needs. This can lead to a people-pleasing behavior that extends beyond the family unit and into other areas of life, such as friendships and romantic relationships. The child learns to prioritize others' needs over their own, a habit that can be difficult to unlearn and hinder the development of a healthy, autonomous self.

In the context of communication, these dynamics create barriers that are not easily dismantled. The child may struggle to articulate their needs or assert boundaries for fear of reprisal or rejection. Conversations about personal goals or life choices can become fraught with tension, as the emotionally immature parent might struggle to engage in a supportive, non-judgmental dialogue.

It is essential for those grappling with these challenges to recognize that the journey toward autonomy is both necessary and deserving of pursuit. It involves setting boundaries, which is not an act of defiance but a step towards healthy self-respect. It requires patience and self-compassion, as the path is often strewn with setbacks and self-doubt. And it may necessitate seeking support from others who can provide the validation and encouragement that the emotionally immature parent cannot offer.

Ultimately, the struggle for autonomy is a testament to the human spirit's resilience. It is about finding one's voice in the face of silence, claiming one's space where there is overreach, and nurturing one's sense of self in an environment that may not always recognize its worth.

It is a profoundly personal yet universally understood aspect of the human experience – the right to define and express oneself freely and authentically.

Chapter Summary

- Emotionally immature parents communicate indirectly, leaving children guessing their intentions and feelings.
- These parents may trivialize their children's emotions, teaching them to doubt and suppress their feelings.
- Blame-shifting is expected, with parents deflecting responsibility to their children instead of accepting accountability.
- Parents use projection to accuse children of having motives or emotions that reflect the parent's issues.
- Communication inconsistency from parents creates an unstable environment, making children feel they must tread carefully.
- Avoidance and denial by parents prevent open dialogue and emotional honesty, leaving children feeling unseen and unheard.
- Conflict and criticism from parents can be disproportionate and defensive, damaging children's self-esteem and sense of self.
- The child's desire for approval complicates the struggle for autonomy, leading to self-censorship and people-pleasing behavior.

5

BOUNDARIES AND EMOTIONAL IMMATURITY

Understanding Boundaries

Boundaries are the invisible lines that define the limits of how we expect to be treated by others. They are essential for healthy relationships and a strong sense of self. When it comes to emotionally immature parents, understanding boundaries becomes exceptionally crucial.

These parents may not recognize or respect their children's boundaries due to their emotional needs and insecurities. This lack of boundary recognition can lead to a dynamic where children feel responsible for their parent's emotional well-being, often at their own expense.

Boundaries are frequently blurred or disregarded in a household where emotional immaturity prevails. Children may find that their personal space, feelings, and thoughts are not given the respect they deserve. This can manifest in parents sharing too much of their issues with their children, expecting their children to cater to their emotional states, or dismissing their children's need for privacy and autonomy.

The establishment of boundaries is a developmental milestone. As children grow, they learn to say 'no' and to understand that their feelings and needs are valid and essential. However, children may struggle to develop this critical skill when a parent does not model healthy boundaries. They may feel that their needs are secondary to their parents' and that asserting themselves is an act of defiance or a cause for guilt.

For children of emotionally immature parents, setting boundaries can be fraught with anxiety. There is often a deeply ingrained fear that asserting their needs will lead to rejection or punishment. This fear can persist into adulthood, making it challenging for these individuals to advocate for themselves in other relationships, whether personal or professional.

Children risk becoming entangled with their parents' emotional states without clear boundaries. This enmeshment can lead to a lack of differentiation, where children need help identifying where their parents' feelings end and begin. As a result, they may become hyper-attuned to the needs and moods of others, often at the cost of their emotional health.

It is also important to note that boundaries are not just about saying no; they are also about saying yes to the things that affirm our well-being. They allow us to choose what we let into our lives and what we keep out. When children learn that their boundaries are not respected, they may also struggle to understand healthy relationships and seek out or maintain those relationships.

Without boundaries, children may develop coping mechanisms that can be detrimental in the long run. They might become people-pleasers, constantly seeking approval and validation from others, or swing to the other extreme, becoming overly rigid and distant to protect themselves from further emotional intrusion.

Understanding boundaries is the first step towards healing from the impact of growing up with emotionally immature parents. It is about recognizing the right to one's feelings, thoughts, and needs. It is about learning to assert oneself in a way that is respectful to both self and others. And ultimately, it is about creating a life where one can thrive, not just survive, despite the challenges of the past.

The Consequences of Poor Boundaries

Children raised by emotionally immature parents may find themselves in the precarious position of navigating a world without clear limits or guidelines. The lack of boundaries can manifest in several ways, each with challenges and repercussions.

One of the most immediate consequences is the role reversal often observed in these families. Children may feel compelled to take on adult responsibilities, becoming caretakers for their parents' emotional well-being. This role reversal sometimes referred to as parentification, can burden a child with undue stress and rob them of a carefree childhood. It can also lead to an underdeveloped sense of self, as the child's needs and desires are consistently sidelined in favor of the parents.

Furthermore, children may need clear boundaries to develop a robust sense of autonomy. They might find it challenging to recognize where they end and others begin, leading to difficulties forming healthy relationships later in life. This enmeshment can result in a lack of personal identity and an over-reliance on others for validation and self-worth.

The emotional volatility often present in homes with emotionally immature parents can also create an environment of unpredictability. Children may become hyper-vigilant, constantly on guard for their parent's next outburst or emotional need. This state of heightened alertness can lead to anxiety and stress, which, if left unchecked, can persist into adulthood.

In addition, the absence of boundaries may leave children vulnerable to manipulation. Emotionally immature parents may use guilt, withdrawal of affection, or other manipulative tactics to maintain control or avoid dealing with their issues. This manipulation can sow seeds of confusion in children, making it difficult to trust their feelings and perceptions.

The consequences of poor boundaries extend beyond the immediate family as well. Social interactions may be fraught with misunderstandings, as these children might either lack the ability to assert themselves or do so in an overly aggressive or confrontational way. The balance of give-and-take in relationships can be elusive, leading to a pattern of one-sided friendships or romantic partnerships.

It is essential to recognize that the impact of growing up with emotionally immature parents is not a life sentence. Awareness is the first step toward change. By understanding the consequences of poor boundaries, individuals can begin the process of healing and growth. They can learn to establish and maintain healthy boundaries, which will be explored in the forthcoming discussion, and in doing so, they can reclaim their sense of self and build more fulfilling relationships.

Setting and Maintaining Healthy Boundaries

In the journey of personal growth, setting and maintaining healthy boundaries emerges as a pivotal skill. Boundaries are the invisible lines we draw around ourselves to protect our well-being and define what is acceptable and not in our relationships. They are essential in fostering respect, understanding, and a sense of individuality.

When dealing with emotionally immature parents, establishing boundaries can be particularly challenging. These parents may have never learned to respect the personal space and autonomy of others, often because their boundaries were not respected during their formative years. As a result, they might intrude upon, dismiss, or even ridicule the boundaries their children attempt to set. This can lead to a cycle of frustration and resentment, which, if left unaddressed, can severely strain the parent-child relationship.

To set boundaries with emotionally immature parents, it is crucial first to identify what you value and need in your relationship with them. Reflect on the areas where you feel discomfort, anger, or sadness. These emotions are often indicators that a boundary has been crossed. It might be the expectation that you will always put their needs before your own or the lack of privacy in your personal life. Once you pinpoint these areas, you can begin articulating your boundaries.

Communicating your boundaries clearly and assertively is the next step. This does not mean being aggressive or confrontational. Instead, it involves expressing your needs calmly and firmly. For example, "I value our time together, but I need some time for myself. Let's schedule our calls once a week instead of every day." It's essential to use "I" statements, which focus on your feelings and needs, rather than "you" statements, which can be accusatory.

Expect resistance. Emotionally immature parents may not readily accept your boundaries. They might react with confusion, anger, or guilt-tripping tactics. It's essential to remain consistent and not to give in to emotional manipulation. This is where maintaining the boundaries you've set becomes vital. Consistency conveys that you are serious about your needs and expect them to be respected.

It can be helpful to establish consequences for boundary violations. These should not be punitive but rather actions you will take to protect your well-being. For instance, if a parent continues to call you multiple times a day after you've asked for space, you might decide not to answer the phone outside of the agreed-upon times.

Self-care is an integral part of maintaining boundaries. It can be emotionally taxing to navigate these dynamics, and nurturing yourself in the process is essential. This might involve seeking support from friends, a therapist, or support groups where you can share your experiences and learn from others who have faced similar challenges.

Remember, setting and maintaining boundaries is not an act of selfishness; it is an act of self-respect. It allows you to engage with your parents from a place of strength and stability rather than compliance and resentment. It is a step towards a healthier, more balanced relationship where both parties can interact with mutual respect and understanding.

Dealing with Resistance

As you embark on the journey of setting and maintaining healthy boundaries with emotionally immature parents, it is almost inevitable that you will encounter resistance. This resistance can manifest in various forms, from subtle guilt-tripping to outright anger and denial. It is a natural reaction, as boundaries can challenge long-standing family dynamics and power structures. Understanding and navigating this resistance is crucial for your emotional well-being and the health of your relationship with your parents.

When dealing with resistance, it's essential to recognize that emotionally immature individuals often struggle with self-reflection and may have a limited capacity for empathy. Their responses to boundary-setting are not necessarily personal attacks but reflections of their emotional regulation and understanding of limitations. They might perceive your boundaries as a form of rejection or criticism, which can trigger defensive behaviors.

One common form of resistance is the emotional plea. Your parent may express hurt feelings or sadness to persuade you to retract your boundaries. While listening and validating genuine emotions is essential, it is equally important to remain firm in your decisions. Compassion does not require you to sacrifice your needs; it means acknowledging their feelings while also honoring your own.

Another form of resistance is denial. Your parent may deny that there is a problem or that your boundaries are necessary. They might insist that you are misinterpreting their actions or being too sensitive. In these instances, having clear examples of behaviors that necessitate the boundaries is helpful. Communicate your experiences calmly and assertively without expecting them to understand or agree immediately.

Sometimes, resistance can escalate to anger or blame. Your parent may accuse you of being selfish, ungrateful, or disrespectful. In the face of such accusations, it is crucial to remain calm and not engage in a power struggle. Reiterate your boundaries, focusing on your needs and feelings, using "I" statements to avoid sounding accusatory.

It's also possible that your parent will test your boundaries, consciously or unconsciously, to see if they are firm. Consistency is critical in these moments. Each time a boundary is tested, calmly reaffirm it. This conveys that your boundaries are not negotiable, and you are committed to upholding them.

Sometimes, you may need to implement consequences if your boundaries are repeatedly disregarded. This could mean reducing contact or taking a break from the relationship until your parent is willing to respect your boundaries. While this can be a painful step to take, it is sometimes necessary for your mental health and the possibility of a healthier relationship in the future.

Remember, setting boundaries is not an act of aggression; it is an act of self-respect and self-care. It is about creating a relationship dynamic for mutual respect and emotional safety. As you navigate the resistance from your emotionally immature parents, it is essential to seek support from friends, therapists, or support groups. They can give you the encouragement and perspective needed to stay the course.

Dealing with resistance is a testament to your strength and commitment to well-being. It is a complex but essential step in fostering a healthier dynamic with your parents, where your emotional needs are acknowledged and respected.

Chapter Summary

- Boundaries define how we expect to be treated; they're crucial for healthy relationships and self-identity, especially with emotionally immature parents who may not respect their children's boundaries.

- Children in homes with emotionally immature parents often experience blurred boundaries, leading to a lack of respect for their personal space, feelings, and autonomy.
- The development of boundaries is a milestone; children with emotionally immature parents may struggle to assert their needs, feeling responsible for their parent's emotions.
- Setting boundaries can cause anxiety for these children, fearing rejection or punishment, and this fear can extend into their adult relationships.
- Without clear boundaries, children risk becoming entangled with their parents' emotions, leading to difficulty differentiating their feelings from their parents'.
- Boundaries are about saying yes to what affirms our well-being; children with poor boundaries may struggle to recognize and maintain healthy relationships.
- Poor boundaries can lead to detrimental coping mechanisms, such as people-pleasing or becoming overly rigid to protect oneself from emotional harm.
- Understanding and asserting boundaries is the first step towards healing from the impact of emotionally immature parents, allowing individuals to thrive despite past challenges.

6

THE EMOTIONAL TOOLBOX

Self-Awareness and Emotional Intelligence

Growing up with emotionally immature parents can often leave children without a clear roadmap for navigating their emotional landscapes. As adults, these children may find themselves at a loss when understanding and managing their feelings. This is where self-awareness and emotional intelligence become a cornerstone for personal growth and healing.

Self-awareness is the ability to recognize and understand your moods, emotions, and drives and their effect on others. On the other hand, emotional intelligence is the capacity to be aware of, control, and express one's emotions and handle interpersonal relationships judiciously and empathetically. Both are essential tools for anyone, but they are particularly vital for those who have experienced the challenges of emotionally immature parenting.

To begin cultivating self-awareness, creating a space for introspection is essential. This can be achieved through journaling, meditation, or therapy. These activities encourage a dialogue with oneself, allowing for a deeper understanding of personal emotional triggers and patterns. Recognizing these patterns is the first step toward change. For instance, you might feel particularly anxious when faced with uncertainty. This trait could stem from the unpredictability of an emotionally immature parent's reactions.

Emotional intelligence involves more than just recognizing your own emotions; it also includes understanding the emotions of others. For those raised by emotionally immature parents, this can be a complex task. These parents may not have modeled empathy or dismissed or invalidated their children's feelings, making it difficult for them to learn how to empathize effectively. However, with conscious effort, one can learn to listen actively and respond to others with sensitivity and understanding.

One practical method to enhance emotional intelligence is practicing active conversation listening. This means fully concentrating on what is being said rather than passively hearing the speaker's message. It involves listening with all senses and giving full attention to the speaker. This practice can help in recognizing the emotions behind words and responding to them appropriately.

Another critical aspect of emotional intelligence is the ability to regulate one's own emotions. This means not only understanding how you feel but also how to respond to those feelings in a way that is constructive rather than destructive. Deep breathing, mindfulness, and cognitive restructuring can help manage emotional responses. For example, when feeling overwhelmed, taking a moment to breathe deeply and center oneself can prevent a reactive and potentially harmful response.

It is also beneficial to cultivate a vocabulary for emotions. Many people raised by emotionally immature parents were not taught how to express their feelings and may struggle to identify what they are feeling beyond basic emotions like happiness, sadness, or anger. Expanding one's emotional vocabulary can provide a more nuanced understanding of one's emotional state, leading to more effective communication and self-regulation.

Developing self-awareness and emotional intelligence is a journey that requires patience, practice, and self-compassion. It is about building skills that can lead to a more fulfilling and emotionally rich life. As you learn to navigate your emotional world with greater ease, you will be better equipped to manage the complexities of relationships, including those with emotionally immature parents.

Managing Emotions

In understanding emotionally immature parents, we have explored the importance of self-awareness and emotional intelligence. Now, let's delve into the practical strategies for managing emotions, which is a critical component of the emotional toolbox we are equipping ourselves with.

Emotionally immature parents often struggle with managing their own emotions, which can lead to a tumultuous family environment. As their child, whether you are an adolescent or an adult, you may find yourself frequently on the receiving end of emotional outbursts or cold indifference. It is essential, then, to learn how to navigate these waters with grace and resilience.

Firstly, it is essential to recognize that you cannot control your parents' emotions. Still, you can control your responses to them. Begin by identifying your emotional triggers and your typical responses to your parents' behaviors. Awareness is the first step towards change, and by understanding your patterns, you can break free from reactive cycles.

Once you grasp your triggers, you can employ techniques to manage your emotional responses. Deep breathing, mindfulness, and meditation are powerful tools that can help calm your nervous system and provide a buffer against immediate reactions. When faced with an emotionally charged situation, take a moment to breathe deeply and center yourself. This pause allows you to choose a more thoughtful and composed response.

Another critical strategy is setting healthy boundaries. Boundaries are not about changing the other person but about respecting your needs and limits. Communicate your boundaries to your parents in a firm yet compassionate manner. It is okay to say no, to ask for space, or to decline participation in conversations that you find emotionally draining.

It is also beneficial to seek out support systems outside of your family. Friends, mentors, support groups, or therapists can provide a sounding board and offer guidance. They can help you process your emotions, reinforce your boundaries, and remind you of your worth when your parents' immaturity makes you question it.

Lastly, practice self-compassion. Growing up with emotionally immature parents can leave you with a harsh inner critic. It is crucial to be kind to yourself, acknowledge your feelings, and recognize that you are doing your best in a challenging situation. Self-compassion is not self-pity; it is about treating yourself with the same kindness and understanding that you would offer a good friend.

By incorporating these strategies into your emotional toolbox, you can cultivate a sense of emotional autonomy and resilience. While you cannot change your parents' past or behavior, you can empower yourself to navigate your emotional world with more excellent skill and confidence. As we build upon these tools, we will explore how empathy can further enhance our relationships and our understanding of emotionally immature parents.

The Power of Empathy

Empathy is vital in the emotional toolbox, especially when dealing with emotionally immature parents. It is the bridge that connects us to another person's inner world, allowing us to understand their feelings and perspectives. When we cultivate empathy, we deepen our emotional intelligence and create a space for healing and understanding in our relationships.

For those who have grown up with emotionally immature parents, empathy might not have been modeled effectively. These parents may have struggled to attune to their children's emotional needs, often because their emotional development was stunted early due to their experiences or inherent personality traits. As a result, their children might have felt misunderstood, invalidated, or emotionally neglected.

However, as adults, we can develop empathy that we may not have received. This begins with self-empathy—recognizing and validating our own emotions. By acknowledging our feelings and treating ourselves with kindness and understanding, we set the groundwork for extending empathy to others, including our parents.

Practicing empathy towards emotionally immature parents does not mean excusing their behaviors or neglecting our boundaries. It means looking beyond their actions to the underlying fears, insecurities, and unmet needs that drive their immaturity. This perspective can help us respond to them with compassion rather than react with frustration or anger.

Empathy also empowers us to communicate more effectively. When we approach conversations with an empathetic mindset, we're more likely to express our thoughts and feelings in a way that can be heard and understood. It can also encourage our parents to open up and share more about their experiences, potentially leading to a more authentic connection.

Moreover, empathy has the power to break the cycle of emotional immaturity. By modeling empathetic behavior, we improve our emotional health and influence those around us. Children who observe empathetic interactions are more likely to develop solid emotional skills, ensuring that the next generation is better equipped to handle the complexities of emotional life.

In embracing empathy, we must also recognize its limits. Sometimes, our empathy may not be reciprocated or appreciated despite our best efforts. In such instances, it's essential to maintain our emotional boundaries and practice self-care. Empathy should not come at the cost of our well-being.

Empathy stands out as a transformative tool as we continue to build our emotional toolbox. It allows us to connect with others more profoundly and fosters a more compassionate world. By integrating empathy into our daily lives, we improve our relationships with emotionally immature parents and enhance our overall emotional resilience and adaptability.

Resilience and Adaptability

Growing up with emotionally immature parents can feel like navigating a ship in unpredictable waters. The unpredictable moods, the lack of emotional support, and the role reversal where the child becomes the caretaker can lead to a tumultuous inner world. However, amidst these challenges lies the opportunity for developing a profound level of resilience and adaptability—two indispensable tools in the emotional toolbox that can be honed to navigate life's complexities.

Resilience is the ability to bounce back from difficulties, recover strength, and progress despite emotional setbacks. For children of emotionally immature parents, resilience becomes a survival skill. The inner force allows them to emerge from the chaos of their upbringing not just intact but often with a unique strength. This strength is characterized by a deep understanding that they can endure much and still find ways to thrive.

Adaptability, on the other hand, is the capacity to adjust to new conditions. When the emotional landscape of home is ever-shifting, adaptability becomes second nature. Children learn to read the room, anticipate the unpredictable, and mold themselves in ways that can minimize conflict or emotional distress. While this skill is developed under less-than-ideal circumstances, it can be a powerful asset later in life, allowing individuals to navigate change with grace and flexibility.

To cultivate resilience, one must first acknowledge the reality of their situation. It involves a conscious decision not to be defined by the limitations of one's parents. This means recognizing that while you cannot change the past, you can influence your reaction to it and your path forward. It is about finding and focusing on the aspects of life you can control, such as your beliefs, choices, and actions.

Building resilience also involves fostering a sense of self-worth independent of parental validation. It means setting personal boundaries and learning to say no, which can be particularly challenging for those who have been conditioned to put their parents' emotional needs first. It's about understanding that self-care is not selfish but essential to maintaining one's emotional health.

Adaptability is enhanced through accepting change as an inherent part of life. It requires a willingness to let go of rigid expectations and embrace the idea that there is more than one way to achieve a goal or to find happiness. For the adult child of emotionally immature parents, it means learning to trust their instincts and make decisions based on their values rather than constantly seeking approval or direction from others.

Resilience and adaptability are nurtured through supportive relationships with friends, mentors, or a therapeutic community. These connections can provide the encouragement and feedback necessary to reinforce an individual's sense of self and to help them navigate the complexities of their emotions and relationships.

In essence, resilience and adaptability are about surviving the storm and learning to dance in the rain. They are about recognizing that while we cannot control the weather, we can adjust our sails. For those who have grown up with emotionally immature parents, these skills are not just theoretical concepts but lived experiences that shape their approach to life's challenges and opportunities.

As we explore the emotional toolbox, it becomes clear that the tools we gather are interconnected. The resilience and adaptability we develop in response to our upbringing can be further enhanced by cultivating mindfulness and presence, allowing us to live more fully in the moment and engage with our lives and relationships more meaningfully.

Mindfulness and Presence

In navigating the complex emotional landscape that comes with having emotionally immature parents, it's essential to develop an array of coping strategies. One such strategy, which can be particularly transformative, is the practice of mindfulness and presence.

Mindfulness is fully engaging with the present moment without judgment or distraction. It is about experiencing life with an open heart and a clear mind as it unfolds. For those who have grown up with emotionally immature parents, mindfulness can be a beacon of stability in the often tumultuous waves of emotional unpredictability.

When practicing mindfulness, we learn to observe our thoughts and feelings without getting entangled. This is crucial when dealing with emotionally immature parents, who may often project their feelings onto us or create an environment where emotional reactions are heightened and unpredictable. By cultivating mindfulness, we can create a space between stimulus and response, allowing us to choose how we react to our parents' behaviors.

Presence, a companion to mindfulness, is about being fully attuned to the here and now. It means engaging with our environment and its people with our full attention. For adults who have emotionally immature parents, presence can be a powerful tool. It allows us to interact with our parents without being hijacked by past grievances or future anxieties. It helps us to maintain our emotional boundaries and engage in conversations without being pulled into old patterns of conflict or emotional neglect.

The practice of mindfulness and presence begins with simple steps. It can be as straightforward as taking a few deep breaths before responding to a parent's comment that might otherwise trigger an automatic reaction. It might involve a daily meditation, where we sit quietly and observe our thoughts, learning to let them pass without attachment. Or it could be a mindful walk, where we focus intently on the sensations of our body moving and the environment around us.

As we become more adept at these practices, we notice a shift in our interactions with our parents. We may be less reactive and more compassionate with them and ourselves. We might discover a newfound patience and a greater capacity for listening and understanding, even when faced with emotional immaturity.

Moreover, mindfulness and presence can help us to appreciate the good moments, no matter how small, and to find joy and gratitude in our relationships. They teach us to live with peace and acceptance, knowing that while we cannot change our parents, we can change our relationship experience.

In essence, mindfulness and presence are not just practices but a way of life—a way to navigate the complex emotional waters with grace, strength, and stability. They are essential tools in our emotional toolbox, helping us build a responsive rather than reactive life grounded in a deep sense of self-awareness and self-care.

Chapter Summary

- Growing up with emotionally immature parents can hinder a child's ability to manage emotions, necessitating the development of self-awareness and emotional intelligence.
- Self-awareness involves recognizing one's emotions and their impact on others. In contrast, emotional intelligence includes understanding and regulating emotions and empathizing with others.
- Cultivating self-awareness can be achieved through introspection practices like journaling, meditation, or therapy, which help identify emotional triggers and patterns.
- Emotional intelligence can be enhanced by practicing active listening and learning to regulate emotional responses using deep breathing and mindfulness techniques.

- Expanding one's emotional vocabulary is essential for those who weren't taught to express their feelings, leading to more effective communication and self-regulation.
- Managing emotions involves recognizing that one cannot control one's parents' emotions but can control one's responses, employing techniques like deep breathing and setting healthy boundaries.
- Empathy is crucial for understanding emotionally immature parents, allowing for compassion and improved communication. Still, it should not come at the cost of one's well-being.
- Resilience and adaptability, developed through challenging upbringings, involve recognizing one's ability to bounce back and adjust to new conditions, supported by healthy relationships and self-care.

7

HEALING FROM EMOTIONAL IMMATURITY

The Journey to Healing

Growing up with emotionally immature parents can leave deep-seated marks that often go unrecognized for years. As adults, the journey to healing from these childhood experiences is necessary and challenging. It requires a compassionate understanding of oneself and the courage to confront and reconcile with the past.

The first step on this path is the acknowledgment of the pain and confusion that emotionally immature parenting can cause. It's essential to recognize that the feelings of neglect, misunderstanding, or emotional abandonment are valid and significant. This recognition is not about assigning blame but about understanding the context of your emotional world.

Once acknowledgment has taken place, the next phase involves self-compassion. It's about offering yourself the kindness and patience you may not have received as a child. Self-compassion is a nurturing practice that allows you to create a safe emotional space for healing. It involves treating yourself with the same care and understanding that you would offer a good friend.

Another vital aspect of healing is setting boundaries. Boundaries are the guidelines you set for yourself and others regarding acceptable behavior. They are crucial in protecting your emotional well-being. For those who have grown up with emotionally immature parents, learning to establish and maintain healthy boundaries can be a transformative experience. It empowers you to control your interactions and advocate for your needs.

Developing emotional literacy is also a vital component of the healing journey. Emotional literacy is identifying, expressing, and managing emotions effectively. It's about becoming fluent in the language of emotions, which may have been discouraged or ignored in your upbringing. By enhancing your emotional literacy, you can better navigate your feelings and the feelings of others, leading to more fulfilling and authentic relationships.

Furthermore, seeking support through therapy or support groups can be an invaluable part of the healing process. A therapist can provide a safe, non-judgmental space to explore your experiences and emotions. They can offer guidance and strategies to help you cope with the lingering effects of emotional immaturity from your parents. Support groups can also offer a sense of community and understanding from others who have had similar experiences.

Lastly, it's essential to cultivate a life that reflects your values, desires, and needs. This might involve pursuing passions previously set aside or creating a chosen family of friends and loved ones who provide the emotional connection and support you deserve. By building a life that honors your true self, you can find fulfillment and joy that extends beyond the shadow of the past.

The journey to healing from the impact of emotionally immature parents is not a linear one. It is filled with complexities and nuances unique to each individual's experiences. However, with each step taken towards understanding, compassion, and self-care, the path becomes more apparent, leading to a more grounded and emotionally resilient self.

Therapeutic Approaches

As we navigate the complexities of healing from the wounds inflicted by emotionally immature parents, it is essential to explore the various therapeutic approaches that can facilitate this profoundly personal journey. These approaches are not one-size-fits-all; they offer a spectrum of strategies tailored to the individual's experiences and needs.

One of the most effective therapeutic approaches is individual psychotherapy. In this confidential space, a trained therapist can help you understand the roots of your emotional pain and the impact of your parents' immaturity on your development. Through techniques such as cognitive-behavioral therapy (CBT), you can learn to challenge and reframe the negative beliefs about yourself that may have been instilled during childhood. CBT can also provide you with tools to cope with anxiety, depression, and other emotional difficulties that often accompany the experience of being raised by emotionally immature parents.

Another approach that has proven beneficial is group therapy. Sharing your story with others with similar experiences can be incredibly validating and empowering. It helps to know you are not alone in your struggles. Group therapy provides a supportive environment where you can learn from the experiences of others, gain different perspectives, and practice new ways of relating to people in a safe setting.

For some, family therapy might be an option, mainly if there is a willingness from the family to acknowledge past issues and work together toward healing. This form of therapy can facilitate open communication, help resolve conflicts, and teach family members healthier ways of interacting with one another. However, it is essential to note that family therapy is not suitable for everyone, especially if there is ongoing abuse or a complete lack of willingness to change from emotionally immature parents.

Mindfulness and meditation practices can also be incorporated into the healing process. These practices help develop a greater awareness of the present moment. They can be instrumental in managing stress and emotional regulation. By observing your thoughts and feelings without judgment, you can break the cycle of reactivity that may have been a survival mechanism in your childhood environment.

Art therapy is another avenue through which many find healing. It offers a non-verbal outlet for expressing complex emotions. It can benefit those who struggle to articulate their feelings through words. Through the creative process, you may discover insights about yourself and your past that were previously obscured.

Lastly, self-help and educational resources can complement therapeutic approaches. Books, workshops, and online content focused on overcoming the challenges of emotionally immature parents can provide additional support and guidance. These resources can help you understand that your experiences are part of a larger narrative shared by many and that recovery is possible and within reach.

Each of these therapeutic approaches can be a stepping stone toward healing. It is important to remember that the process is not linear and may require trying different methods to find what resonates with you. The ultimate goal is to build a life defined not by the limitations of the past but by the possibilities of a future where emotional maturity and well-being are within your control.

Forgiveness and Letting Go

In the journey toward healing,, there comes a pivotal moment when one must confront the concept of forgiveness and the act of letting go. This is not a straightforward path, nor is it one that can be rushed or prescribed in a uniform way for everyone. However, it is crucial to reclaim one's emotional well-being and autonomy.

In this context, forgiveness is not about condoning the hurtful behavior of parents who may have been emotionally unavailable or erratic. It is not about absolving them of responsibility or pretending that the pain they caused did not matter. Instead, forgiveness is an internal process, releasing the burden of carrying anger, resentment, or a desire for retribution. It is a personal liberation from the emotional shackles that bind one to the past.

Forgiveness is acknowledging the whole reality of what occurred and accepting that it cannot be changed. It is to understand that emotionally immature parents, in many cases, were limited by their psychological struggles and may not have been capable of providing the emotional support their children needed. This understanding does not excuse their actions but provides a context that can help mitigate the sting of personal insult.

Letting go is the natural companion to forgiveness. It involves the conscious decision to stop allowing past grievances to dictate one's emotional state and life choices. Letting go shifts focus from what has been lost to what can be created anew. It is about moving forward with the lessons learned and the strength gained from surviving and transcending past adversity.

The process of forgiveness and letting go is deeply personal and often nonlinear. It may involve moments of profound insight and periods of backsliding into old patterns of resentment. It is essential to approach this process with patience and self-compassion, understanding that healing is not a destination but a continual journey.

As one works through these emotional complexities, engaging in practices that nurture the self and reinforce the commitment to personal growth is helpful. These may include mindfulness meditation, journaling, or creative expression—anything that allows for reflection and the constructive processing of emotions.

Ultimately, forgiveness and letting go are acts of self-care. They free individuals from the weight of past hurts and empower them to build a life defined not by what has been endured but by what one chooses to cultivate in its aftermath. This is the foundation upon which one can begin to rebuild the self, constructing an identity rooted in the present and looking toward the future with hope and resilience.

Rebuilding the Self

Growing up with emotionally immature parents can leave deep imprints on one's sense of self. The journey of healing is not just about moving past the pain but also about reconstructing a self-identity that may have been neglected or distorted through years of emotional turbulence. This reconstruction is a process of self-discovery, self-compassion, and self-empowerment.

The first step in rebuilding the self is to understand that your worth is not contingent on the approval or understanding of your parents. This is a challenging realization for many, as the desire for parental validation is deeply ingrained. It's important to acknowledge that your value is intrinsic and not dependent on someone else's ability to recognize it.

Self-discovery involves exploring your interests, desires, and values independent of your parents' influence. It's about asking yourself who you are outside of the role you played in your family. This can be both liberating and daunting, as it may involve entering unfamiliar territory. It's okay to start small, with simple questions like what colors you prefer, what hobbies you enjoy, or what causes you feel passionate about. Over time, these small discoveries can build a more comprehensive picture of your authentic self.

Self-compassion is crucial in this journey. You may have internalized critical voices from your parents, which can lead to self-doubt and self-criticism. Learning to speak to yourself with kindness and understanding is vital to healing. This might involve challenging negative self-talk, practicing mindfulness, or engaging in activities that make you feel nurtured and cared for. Remember, healing is not a linear process, and it's okay to have days where you feel less than your best.

Self-empowerment comes from setting boundaries and advocating for your needs. Emotionally immature parents may not have respected your boundaries in the past. Still, as an adult, you have the right to establish what is acceptable for you. This might mean saying no to demands that compromise your well-being, asking for space, or seeking out reciprocal and respectful relationships. Empowerment also means recognizing that you have the agency to shape your life and make choices that align with your true self.

As you engage in this rebuilding process, seeking out support is essential. This can come from friends, a therapist, support groups, or any safe space where you can express your feelings and experiences without judgment. Surrounding yourself with understanding individuals can provide encouragement and perspective as you navigate the complexities of healing.

In rebuilding the self, you are not erasing your past or the influence of your parents. Instead, you are using what you've learned from your experiences to forge a stronger, more resilient sense of self. You are acknowledging the child you once were, with all their needs and feelings, and committing to being the nurturing presence that child deserves. This is not a journey of forgetting but one of transformation and growth, where the scars of the past become the wisdom of the present.

Creating New Family Dynamics

In the journey toward healing from the wounds inflicted by emotionally immature parents, we have traversed the rugged terrain of self-reconstruction. With newfound strength and self-awareness, we now turn our attention to the delicate task of reshaping the family dynamics that have, for so long, been defined by emotional immaturity.

Creating new family dynamics is not about changing others—futile and outside our control—but changing how we engage with our family.

It is about establishing boundaries, communicating effectively, and nurturing our emotional health in the context of these relationships.

The first step in this transformative process is recognizing and accepting that our parents may never fully understand or validate our feelings. This can be a painful realization, but it is also a liberating one. It allows us to stop seeking approval and build a sense of independence from our parents' perceptions.

Next, we must learn the art of boundary-setting. Boundaries are not walls meant to shut others out; they are gates that allow us to interact with others on our terms. They help us to define what is acceptable and what is not, what we are willing to tolerate, and what we are not. When we establish clear boundaries, we communicate to our parents and ourselves that our feelings and needs are valid and essential.

Effective communication is the cornerstone of any relationship, and this holds especially true in the context of emotionally charged family dynamics. We must strive to express our thoughts and feelings calmly and clearly without expecting our parents to always respond in the way we hope. It is also crucial to listen actively, trying to understand our parents' perspective, even if we disagree. This does not mean we condone their emotional immaturity, but rather that we acknowledge it as a part of the reality we must navigate.

Creating new family dynamics may mean limiting contact or taking time away from family interactions. This is not an act of malice but one of self-preservation. It is about giving ourselves the space to grow and heal without being constantly pulled back into the chaos of emotional immaturity.

Finally, it is essential to cultivate a support system outside of our family. Friends, mentors, therapists, and support groups can provide the understanding and encouragement we may not receive from our parents. They can offer perspectives and advice that help us to see our family situation more clearly and to navigate it more effectively.

In creating new family dynamics, we are not discarding our past but redefining our present and future. We are not abandoning our family but are engaging with them in a healthier, more self-respecting manner. This is not a journey we undertake lightly, but it promises a more authentic and fulfilling life. As we continue to heal and grow, we can find peace in the knowledge that we have the power to shape our own lives, regardless of where we started.

Chapter Summary

- Acknowledge the pain caused by emotionally immature parents and understand that feelings of neglect and emotional abandonment are valid.
- Practice self-compassion by offering yourself kindness and patience, creating a safe emotional space for healing.
- Set boundaries to protect emotional well-being and take control of interactions, advocating for personal needs.
- Develop emotional literacy to identify, express, and manage emotions, leading to more authentic relationships.
- Seek support through therapy or support groups to explore emotions and cope with the effects of emotional immaturity.
- Cultivate a life that reflects personal values, desires, and needs, pursuing passions and creating a supportive chosen family.
- Explore various therapeutic approaches tailored to individual needs, such as individual psychotherapy, group therapy, and mindfulness.
- Engage in forgiveness and letting go as acts of self-care, releasing the burden of anger and resentment to move forward.

8

NAVIGATING RELATIONSHIPS WITH EMOTIONALLY IMMATURE PARENTS

Reevaluating the Parent-Child Relationship

In the journey of personal growth, there comes a pivotal moment where reevaluating the parent-child relationship becomes beneficial and necessary. This reevaluation is a process of understanding that the dynamics established in childhood may no longer serve your well-being as an adult. It is a step towards emotional autonomy and healthier interactions.

As you embark on this reevaluation, it is essential to approach it with a blend of honesty and compassion. Begin by acknowledging the reality of your parents' emotional capabilities. Emotionally immature parents often struggle with self-awareness and empathy, which can manifest in their inability to engage in deep, meaningful conversations or to provide the emotional support they may seek. Recognizing these limitations is not an act of condemnation but rather an acceptance of who they are. This acceptance allows you to set realistic expectations for your relationship with them.

In this process, reflecting on how your parents' emotional immaturity has shaped your emotional responses and behaviors is crucial. Have you found yourself adopting specific roles to cope with their immaturity? Perhaps you've become the caretaker, the peacekeeper, or the one who always compromises to avoid conflict. Identifying these patterns can enlighten and empower you to make conscious choices about how you interact with your parents moving forward.

Another aspect of reevaluation is considering the boundaries you need to establish for your mental and emotional well-being. Boundaries are not about pushing your parents away but protecting your inner peace. They can range from deciding how often you communicate with your parents to what topics you choose to discuss with them. Setting boundaries is an act of self-care and is essential in any relationship, especially those with emotionally immature individuals.

As you redefine your relationship with your parents, seeking out and fostering other supportive relationships is equally important. Surrounding yourself with friends, mentors, or counselors who understand and respect your emotional needs can provide a contrast to the dynamics you experience with your parents. These relationships can offer the empathy and maturity that you may not receive from your parents, and they can be a source of strength and validation.

Lastly, it is essential to practice self-compassion throughout this reevaluation. You may experience various emotions, from sadness and anger to relief and hope. These feelings are all valid. Reevaluating your relationship with your parents is not a straightforward path, and it may involve periods of trial and error. Be patient with yourself as you navigate this complex terrain.

By reevaluating your relationship with your parents, you are taking a courageous step toward creating a life that honors your emotional needs and well-being. Remember, this reevaluation is not about finding fault or assigning blame but about understanding the dynamics at play and making informed decisions on how to interact with your parents in a way that is healthiest for you.

Communication Strategies

Communication is a pivotal element in the journey of understanding and interacting with emotionally immature parents. It is a delicate dance that requires patience, clarity, and, often, a redefinition of expectations. The strategies discussed here aim to foster a constructive dialogue, given the unique challenges that emotionally immature parents may present.

Firstly, it is essential to approach conversations with a sense of calm and self-assuredness. Emotionally immature parents may not respond well to confrontation or heightened emotions. Therefore, grounding yourself before engaging in discussions can help maintain a serenity conducive to productive communication.

One effective strategy is to employ "I" statements. This technique involves speaking from your perspective without casting blame. For instance, instead of saying, "You never listen to me," you might say, "I feel unheard when I share my thoughts with you." This approach can minimize defensiveness and open the door to more empathetic exchanges.

Active listening is another critical component. This means genuinely hearing your parents' words without immediately formulating a response or judgment. Reflecting on what you've heard them say can validate their feelings and show that you are engaged in the conversation. For example, "It sounds like you're saying you felt overwhelmed when that happened" can demonstrate understanding and care.

Setting boundaries is often necessary when dealing with emotionally immature parents. It's essential to communicate your limits clearly and consistently. Suppose a conversation becomes too heated or unproductive. In that case, it's okay to say, "I need to step back from this discussion right now, but I'm open to revisiting it later when we're both feeling calmer."

Sometimes, shifting the focus from emotional depth to more practical matters may be beneficial. Emotionally immature parents may struggle with deep emotional conversations, so discussing day-to-day topics or problem-solving can be a way to maintain connection without delving into areas that might trigger conflict or discomfort.

It is also crucial to manage your expectations. You may need to accept that your parents might not be capable of the level of emotional maturity or understanding you desire. This acceptance doesn't mean you lower your standards for how you deserve to be treated, but rather that you recognize the limitations of the relationship and adjust your approach accordingly.

Lastly, consider seeking support for yourself. Whether through therapy, support groups, or trusted friends, having a space to process your feelings and experiences can be invaluable. It can also provide additional strategies and perspectives on navigating the complex terrain of your relationship with your parents.

Communicating with emotionally immature parents requires compassion, self-awareness, and resilience. By employing these strategies, you can create a space for dialogue that respects both your needs and the limitations of your parents' emotional capacities. Remember, the goal is not to change who they are but to find a respectful way to interact and maintain your well-being.

When to Maintain Contact

In the previous section, we explored the delicate art of communication. Let's turn our attention to the considerations that might lead us to maintain contact with our parents despite the challenges their emotional immaturity can present.

Maintaining contact with emotionally immature parents is a deeply personal decision, often rooted in a complex interplay of familial duty, affection, and hope for change. It's essential to recognize that the choice to stay connected does not signify weakness or a lack of awareness. Instead, it can affirm one's values and the desire to uphold family bonds, even when frayed.

One of the primary reasons to maintain contact is the presence of unconditional love. Love, in its purest form, can sometimes transcend the difficulties of emotional immaturity. Your love for your parents motivates you to stay in touch, and this contact does not significantly harm your well-being. This can be a valid reason to sustain the relationship.

Another consideration is the potential for growth and healing. While emotionally immature parents may struggle with change, it is not entirely impossible. With the right communication strategies and boundaries in place, there may be opportunities for small shifts in the relationship dynamics that can lead to more positive interactions over time.

For some, the decision to maintain contact is influenced by practical reasons. This can include financial interdependence, co-parenting grandchildren, or managing family businesses. In such scenarios, contact is not just a personal choice but a practical necessity. Navigating these waters requires a clear set of boundaries and understanding one's limits to prevent emotional drain.

The concept of filial responsibility, deeply ingrained in many cultures, often plays a significant role in the decision to stay connected. The sense of duty to care for one's parents as they age can be a powerful motivator. Suppose this sense of obligation is part of your value system. In that case, finding a balance that honors your beliefs and protects your emotional health is essential.

Lastly, maintaining contact may come from a place of compassion. Recognizing that emotionally immature parents are often dealing with their unresolved issues can lead to a sense of empathy. While this doesn't excuse their behavior, it can provide a context that makes continued contact more manageable.

In all these considerations, assessing this relationship's impact on your life is crucial. It's about finding the proper distance that allows you to engage in a healthy way. This may mean setting firm boundaries, limiting the frequency of contact, or choosing the settings in which you interact with your parents.

Remember, maintaining contact is not about enduring pain for the sake of connection. It's about making an informed choice that aligns with your needs, values, and circumstances. It's a dynamic process that may evolve, requiring you to be reflective and adaptable.

As we move forward, we'll consider the other side of this coin: when it might be necessary to create distance from emotionally immature parents. This is a challenging path to walk, but sometimes, it's necessary for personal well-being and growth.

When to Consider Distance

One of the most challenging decisions you may face is determining whether to create distance in your relationship with emotionally immature parents. This choice is deeply personal and can be fraught with guilt, confusion, and a sense of obligation. However, there are circumstances where establishing boundaries by incorporating distance can be a necessary step for your emotional well-being.

Distance does not necessarily mean cutting off all contact. It can manifest as taking a step back to evaluate the relationship dynamics, reducing the frequency of interactions, or setting firm boundaries around topics of conversation and forms of behavior you find detrimental. The decision to consider distance should be based on a clear understanding of your needs and the patterns of interaction that have historically taken place between you and your parents.

One of the primary reasons to consider distance is the presence of ongoing emotional pain or trauma that is exacerbated by interactions with your parents. Suppose you find yourself repeatedly hurt, disappointed, or emotionally drained after spending time with them. In that case, it may indicate that the relationship impedes your ability to heal and grow.

Another sign that distance may be beneficial is a consistent lack of respect for your boundaries. Emotionally immature parents may struggle with recognizing and honoring their adult children's personal space, beliefs, and choices. Suppose conversations and visits routinely leave you feeling disrespected or violated in your autonomy. In that case, it is worth considering whether the relationship in its current form is healthy for you.

Additionally, notice a pattern of manipulation or emotional blackmail, such as guilt-tripping or passive-aggressive behavior. It may be time to reassess the relationship. These tactics can be particularly damaging, as they often exploit the child's desire for parental approval and love.

It's also important to acknowledge the impact of your parents' emotional immaturity on your other relationships. If maintaining close contact with your parents is causing strain in your romantic partnership, friendships, or parenting, it may be necessary to contemplate distance to protect these other vital connections in your life.

When contemplating distance, it is essential to approach the decision with compassion—not only for yourself but also for your parents. Recognize that their emotional immaturity is likely a result of their unmet needs and unresolved issues. While this understanding does not excuse hurtful behavior, it can help you approach the situation with empathy, reducing the likelihood of unnecessary conflict as you establish boundaries.

It is also crucial to seek support during this time. Whether from friends, a therapist, or a support group, having a network of understanding individuals can give you the strength and perspective to make the best decision for your mental and emotional health.

Ultimately, considering distance is about honoring your needs and nurturing your well-being. It is a step towards breaking the cycle of emotional immaturity and creating a life that is defined not by past pain but by the possibility of a healthier, more fulfilling future.

The Role of Family Therapy

One may reach a point where professional guidance becomes a beacon of hope. Family therapy, a form of psychotherapy that aims to nurture change and development within the family system, can be a valuable resource. It provides a safe space for family members to express their thoughts and feelings. At the same time, a therapist helps navigate the complex emotional landscape.

For those grappling with the challenges posed by emotionally immature parents, family therapy offers a structured environment where each person's perspective is heard and validated. The therapist, trained in managing dynamics where emotional immaturity is present, can facilitate conversations that might otherwise be fraught with misunderstanding and hurt.

In this therapeutic setting, the focus is not on assigning blame but on understanding each family member's emotional world. Emotionally immature parents may struggle with self-awareness and empathy, which can lead to a lack of emotional attunement with their children. A family therapist can help parents explore their childhood experiences, which may have contributed to their emotional development, and how these experiences are reflected in their parenting style.

For adult children, family therapy can be an avenue to articulate their needs and experiences without the fear of retribution or dismissal. It can empower them to establish boundaries and communicate effectively, often for the first time. The therapist can introduce concepts such as emotional intelligence and self-regulation, essential for healthy relationships.

Moreover, family therapy can assist in breaking the cycle of emotional immaturity. By learning new ways of relating and understanding the emotional cues of others, parents can begin to model more mature behaviors. This, in turn, can create a ripple effect, fostering a more emotionally intelligent and resilient family unit.

However, it is essential to note that success in family therapy requires willingness and openness from all parties involved. Emotionally immature parents must be willing to engage in the process and consider the possibility of change. Without this foundational commitment, therapy may become another battleground for family conflict.

In cases where parents are resistant or unable to participate in therapy, individual therapy for the adult child can still be beneficial. It can give them the tools to manage their relationship with their parents and protect their emotional well-being.

Ultimately, family therapy is not a magic cure for the challenges posed by emotionally immature parents. It is a step towards understanding, healing, and possibly transforming strained relationships into ones that are more fulfilling and less fraught with emotional pain. With the guidance of a compassionate therapist, families can embark on a path of growth that honors the complexity of their shared history while forging a healthier emotional future.

Chapter Summary

- Reevaluating the parent-child relationship is crucial for personal growth, especially with emotionally immature parents, to achieve emotional autonomy.
- Acknowledge the limitations of emotionally immature parents, such as a lack of empathy and self-awareness, to set realistic expectations for the relationship.
- Reflect on how your parents' emotional immaturity has influenced your behaviors, like adopting roles of caretaker or peacekeeper, to empower future interactions.
- Establish boundaries for mental and emotional well-being, which is an act of self-care and necessary in relationships with emotionally immature individuals.
- Seek supportive relationships with friends, mentors, or counselors to provide the empathy and maturity lacking in parental relationships.
- Practice self-compassion throughout the reevaluation process, as it involves a range of emotions and is not a straightforward path.

- Communication with emotionally immature parents requires calmness, self-assuredness, strategies like "I" statements, and active listening to foster constructive dialogue.
- Maintaining contact with emotionally immature parents is a personal decision influenced by love, hope for change, practical reasons, cultural duty, and compassion. Still, it requires regular assessment and boundaries to ensure personal well-being.

9

PARENTING AFTER EMOTIONAL IMMATURITY

Breaking the Cycle

The parenting journey is often a mirror, reflecting not just the joys and successes but also the challenges and unresolved issues of our upbringing. For those who have experienced the perplexity and pain of being raised by emotionally immature parents, the path forward can be fraught with uncertainty. How does one ensure that the cycle of emotional immaturity is not perpetuated into the next generation? The answer lies in consciously cultivating emotional intelligence within oneself, thereby rewriting the familial narrative.

Emotional intelligence, at its core, is the ability to recognize, understand, and manage our own emotions and recognize, understand, and influence the emotions of others. It is the cornerstone of healthy, responsive parenting. To break the cycle of emotional immaturity, it is essential to develop the skills that perhaps our parents lacked: empathy, emotional regulation, and the ability to foster secure attachments.

The first step in this transformative process is self-reflection. Take the time to delve into your emotional landscape. Acknowledge the feelings that arise from your childhood experiences, and understand how they have shaped your behavior and reactions. This is not an exercise in blame but rather an opportunity for growth. By identifying the patterns you wish to change, you set the stage for intentional parenting.

Next, commit to learning about and practicing emotional regulation. This means finding healthy ways to cope with stress, frustration, and anger. It involves recognizing when you are becoming emotionally overwhelmed and having strategies to calm yourself. This could be through mindfulness, deep breathing exercises, or even seeking the support of a therapist. As you model emotional regulation, you teach your children to do the same, equipping them with valuable tools for their emotional well-being.

Empathy is another vital component. Strive to see the world through your child's eyes. Validate their feelings, even if they seem trivial to you. Remember, their emotions are as accurate and significant to them as yours are to you. By acknowledging and respecting your child's feelings, you foster an environment of trust and understanding. This empathetic approach allows children to feel heard and supported, which is instrumental in their emotional development.

Lastly, creating secure attachments with your children is paramount. This means being consistently present, both physically and emotionally. It's about offering comfort and security so they know they can rely on you. It's about being responsive to their needs and showing unconditional love. A secure attachment forms the foundation of a child's confidence and self-esteem, which are critical for their journey through life.

Breaking the cycle of emotional immaturity is not an overnight endeavor. It requires patience, dedication, and a willingness to confront and heal from one's past. But the rewards are immeasurable. Not only do you give your children the gift of a nurturing, emotionally intelligent upbringing, but you also heal yourself in the process. As you embark on this path, remember that you are not alone. Support is available through friends, family, or professionals who can guide you along this transformative journey.

As we move forward, we will explore the principles of emotionally intelligent parenting in greater depth. By embracing these principles, you can ensure your children grow up with the emotional skills and resilience they need to thrive in an ever-changing world.

Emotionally Intelligent Parenting

Let's now shift our focus to the cultivation of emotional intelligence within parenting. Emotionally intelligent parenting is not merely a set of actions but a transformation of being, a conscious choice to foster an environment where emotional growth is as valued as intellectual and physical development.

Emotionally intelligent parenting begins with self-awareness. As a parent, recognizing your emotional state is crucial. It's about understanding your triggers, your strengths, and your limitations. This self-knowledge is the bedrock upon which you can build a stable and nurturing environment for your children. When you are aware of your emotional landscape, you can prevent immaturity from spilling over into your parenting style.

Communication is the next pillar of emotionally intelligent parenting. It involves listening with empathy and responding with clarity. Children raised by emotionally intelligent parents feel heard and understood. They are allowed to express their emotions without fear of judgment or dismissal. This open line of communication fosters trust and strengthens the parent-child bond.

Emotional regulation is another critical component. Parents who can manage their emotions model their children to do the same. It's not about suppressing feelings but about expressing them healthily and constructively. When children witness their parents navigating emotions gracefully, they learn to handle their emotional experiences with similar finesse.

Consistency in emotional responses is also vital. Children thrive on predictability, and when parents are consistent in their emotional reactions, it creates a sense of security. This doesn't mean you won't have bad days or moments of frustration. Still, it's about striving to handle these moments with a consistent approach that doesn't leave children feeling unstable or confused.

Finally, fostering empathy in your children is a gift that will serve them throughout their lives. By showing empathy to your children and others, you teach them to do the same. Empathy allows children to connect with others deeply emotionally, leading to more meaningful relationships and a greater understanding of the world around them.

Emotionally intelligent parenting is not an endpoint but a journey. It requires patience, dedication, and a willingness to grow alongside your children. By embracing these principles, you can give your children the tools they need to navigate the complexities of their emotions and the world. In doing so, you are raising emotionally healthy children and healing any remnants of emotional immaturity that may have been passed down through generations.

The Importance of Role Modeling

Role modeling is a beacon of transformation in redefining parenthood, especially after experiencing emotional immaturity from one's parents. Through our daily actions, responses, and decisions, children learn the most about navigating life's complexities. The silent lessons imparted by a parent's behavior often speak louder than any words of wisdom that might be shared around the dinner table.

Role modeling is not about striving for perfection but embracing authenticity and a willingness to grow. When parents exhibit the courage to acknowledge their emotions, manage them responsibly, and communicate effectively, they set a powerful example for their children. This demonstration of emotional intelligence lays the groundwork for children to develop their emotional maturity.

Consider the everyday scenarios where role modeling can have a profound impact. When a parent faces a setback at work and discusses the situation at home, they teach resilience, not with despair or avoidance but with a reflective and proactive attitude. When a parent apologizes after a moment of impatience, they teach accountability and the value of repairing relationships.

It is also in the quiet moments that role modeling takes shape. How a parent treats themselves with kindness and self-care teaches children about self-worth and the importance of personal well-being. The way parents interact with others, showing empathy and respect, even in challenging situations, offers a live demonstration of social skills that books and lectures alone cannot convey.

Moreover, role modeling extends beyond the emotional realm. It encompasses the values and ethics parents wish to instill in their children. By living these values, parents make them tangible for their children. Children are more likely to internalize these qualities, whether honesty, diligence, generosity or any other virtue when they see them in action.

In overcoming emotional immaturity, role modeling becomes even more significant. It is an opportunity to break dysfunction cycles and chart a new course for family dynamics. Parents who consciously model healthy emotional behaviors provide their children with a blueprint for emotional competence. This, in turn, can foster an environment where children feel safe to express themselves, learn from their experiences, and build strong, nurturing relationships.

Embracing the role of a model for emotional maturity is challenging. It requires introspection, a commitment to personal growth, and the humility to recognize that, as parents, we are also lifelong learners. Yet, the rewards of this endeavor are immeasurable. Through our example, we can empower our children to lead emotionally rich and fulfilling lives, equipped with the tools to navigate their relationships and personal challenges gracefully and confidently.

As we explore the facets of parenting after emotional immaturity, it becomes clear that the environment we create for our children is as crucial as the example we set. Within a nurturing environment, the seeds of emotional intelligence, sown by role modeling, can flourish.

Creating a Nurturing Environment

Creating a nurturing environment is one of the most pivotal steps in the parenting journey after emotional immaturity. This environment is not just a physical space but an emotional sanctuary that fosters growth, understanding, and connection. It is where children feel safe to express themselves, explore their identities, and develop resilience against life's adversities.

To cultivate such an environment, it is essential to establish clear and consistent boundaries. Boundaries are not barriers; they are the framework within which children can safely navigate their world. They provide a sense of security and predictability, essential for children who may have experienced the confusion and unpredictability of emotionally immature parenting. Communicating boundaries with kindness and clarity is crucial, ensuring they are age-appropriate and flexible enough to adapt to the child's growing needs.

Active listening plays a vital role in creating a nurturing environment. It involves giving full attention to the child, acknowledging their feelings without judgment, and validating their experiences. When children feel heard, they develop trust and are likelier to approach their parents for guidance and support. This practice also models for children how to listen to others, fostering empathy and social skills.

Emotional availability is another cornerstone of a nurturing environment. Being emotionally available means being present and responsive to a child's emotional needs. It requires parents to be attuned to their emotional states and to manage them effectively to be the steady presence their children need. This does not mean that parents must be perfect; instead, it is about being genuine and willing to own up to and learn from mistakes. This transparency can help children understand that it is okay to be imperfect and that growth is always possible.

Encouraging play and creativity is also essential. Play is children's language and a powerful tool for learning and expression. It allows children to explore different scenarios, practice problem-solving, and express their emotions in a safe context. Creative activities such as drawing, music, and storytelling can be therapeutic and help children process their feelings nonverbally.

Lastly, nurturing an environment of growth also means fostering independence. This involves encouraging children to make choices, take on age-appropriate responsibilities, and learn from the natural consequences of their actions. It is about guiding rather than controlling, allowing children to develop a sense of self-efficacy and confidence in their abilities.

Creating a nurturing environment is an ongoing process that requires patience, reflection, and a willingness to grow alongside your children. It is about building a foundation of love, respect, and understanding to support them throughout their lives. As parents work to provide this nurturing space, they heal the wounds of their past and lay the groundwork for their children's future well-being.

Support Systems and Resources

In redefining one's parenting after experiencing emotional immaturity from one's parents, it is essential to recognize that no individual is an island. The path to becoming a nurturing and emotionally attuned parent is often paved with the support of others. This support can come from various sources, each offering unique assistance and encouragement.

One of the most valuable resources for those seeking to break the cycle of emotional immaturity is therapy or counseling. A qualified mental health professional can provide a safe space to explore one's childhood experiences, understand their impact, and develop strategies for emotional growth. Therapists who specialize in family dynamics and intergenerational trauma can be particularly helpful, as they are equipped to address the specific challenges that come with this territory.

Support groups are another resource that can be immensely beneficial. Connecting with others who have had similar experiences can reduce isolation and provide a sense of community. Within these groups, individuals can share their struggles and successes, offering and receiving advice on navigating the complexities of parenting after emotional immaturity. These groups may exist within local communities or online, providing flexibility and accessibility to those in need.

Educational resources also play a critical role in the healing and growth process. Books, workshops, and seminars focusing on emotional intelligence, parenting skills, and personal development can offer insights and tools not instinctively known to someone who grew up with emotionally immature parents. Learning about healthy parent-child dynamics and effective communication techniques can empower individuals to create the nurturing environment they strive for in their families.

It is also important to cultivate personal relationships that foster growth and healing. Friends, family members, or mentors who understand and support one's journey can provide emotional sustenance. These relationships can offer practical help, such as childcare or advice, as well as emotional support, like validation and encouragement. Having at least one person who believes in one's ability to change and grow can make a significant difference.

Professional resources such as child psychologists or family therapists can be invaluable for parents looking to provide their children with the emotional support they may not have received. These professionals can assist in identifying the emotional needs of children and offer guidance on how to meet those needs effectively.

Lastly, self-care should be noticed as a resource. Parenting is a demanding task, and it is even more challenging for those working to heal their emotional wounds and taking time for themselves through meditation, exercise, or quiet reflection. Self-care ensures one has the emotional and physical energy to be present and responsive to their children's needs.

In summary, while the legacy of emotional immaturity from one's parents can be a heavy burden, there is a wealth of support systems and resources available to help lift that weight. By seeking out and utilizing these resources, individuals can heal themselves and provide their children with the emotionally rich upbringing they deserve.

Chapter Summary

- Breaking the cycle of emotional immaturity in parenting requires developing emotional intelligence, including empathy, emotional regulation, and secure attachments.
- Self-reflection on one's emotional past and learning emotional regulation strategies are critical steps toward intentional and responsive parenting.
- Empathy towards children's feelings and creating secure attachments are crucial for their emotional development and self-esteem.
- Emotionally intelligent parenting involves self-awareness, effective communication, and consistency in emotional responses to foster trust and security.
- Role modeling healthy emotional behaviors is essential for teaching children emotional maturity and resilience.
- A nurturing environment for children includes clear boundaries, active listening, emotional availability, encouragement of play and creativity, and fostering independence.
- Support systems such as therapy, support groups, educational resources, and personal relationships are vital for parents overcoming emotional immaturity.
- Self-care is an essential resource for parents, ensuring they have the emotional and physical energy to be present and responsive to their children's needs.

10

SOCIETAL IMPLICATIONS AND MOVING FORWARD

The Broader Impact of Emotional Immaturity

Emotional immaturity in parents is not an isolated phenomenon, nor does it solely affect the immediate family dynamics. Its ripples extend far beyond the confines of the home, touching upon various facets of society in subtle yet profound ways. The broader impact of such emotional immaturity can be observed in educational systems, workplaces, and even in the broader cultural narratives that shape our understanding of parenting and personal development.

In educational settings, teachers and counselors often encounter the indirect consequences of emotionally immature parenting. Children from such backgrounds may exhibit a range of behaviors, from heightened anxiety and difficulty with peer relationships to challenges with authority and a lack of self-regulation. These behaviors can disrupt classrooms and require additional resources and attention, impacting not only the child in question but also their peers and educators.

Within the workplace, adults who grew up with emotionally immature parents might struggle with professional relationships and self-esteem. They may struggle to navigate constructive criticism, manage stress effectively, or assert themselves healthily. These difficulties can lead to a less cohesive work environment. They may even affect the overall productivity and well-being of employees.

On a societal level, emotionally immature parenting perpetuates a cycle of emotional dysfunction that can hinder the development of emotional intelligence—a key component in fostering a compassionate and progressive society. When emotional immaturity is modeled and normalized, it becomes more difficult for subsequent generations to develop the emotional skills necessary to build strong, resilient communities.

Furthermore, the media often portrays parenting in a way that either idealizes or vilifies the role, with little attention given to the nuanced reality of raising children. This can create unrealistic expectations and perpetuate stigma, making it harder for parents to seek help or for children to understand and address their experiences.

The cost of emotional immaturity in parents is not just a personal or familial issue; it is also an economic one. Mental health services, social support programs, and educational interventions require significant investment, and the lack of emotional skills can lead to increased reliance on such services. By addressing the problem's root—helping parents develop emotional maturity—we can reduce the long-term financial burden on these systems.

As we move forward, it is essential to recognize the pervasive nature of this issue and the importance of addressing it not just in homes but as a collective societal challenge. By changing the narrative around emotional maturity, we can begin to break the cycle and lay the groundwork for healthier, more emotionally intelligent future generations. This involves creating spaces for open dialogue, providing resources for parents and children alike, and reshaping cultural expectations to value emotional growth as a lifelong journey.

Changing the Narrative

In the fabric of our society, the stories we tell ourselves about parenting and emotional maturity are deeply woven into the collective consciousness. Cultural norms, societal expectations, and generational beliefs have historically shaped these narratives. However, as we become more aware of the complexities of human psychology and the pivotal role of emotional development, it is time for us to reexamine and reshape these stories for the betterment of future generations.

Emotionally immature parents, often through no fault of their own, may have been raised in environments where emotional expression was discouraged or even punished. This cycle of emotional suppression is perpetuated when these individuals, in turn, become parents themselves, lacking the tools to foster emotional intelligence in their children. The narrative has long been that parents are infallible figures of authority. Still, this view does not account for the human element of parenting —the vulnerabilities, the uncertainties, and the capacity for growth.

Changing the narrative means acknowledging that emotional immaturity is not a static trait but a dynamic one that can be addressed and improved upon with awareness and effort. It means recognizing that parents, like their children, are on a journey of emotional development that may require support, education, and sometimes, intervention.

To move forward, we must cultivate a culture that values emotional intelligence as a critical parenting component. This involves creating spaces for open dialogue about the emotional challenges of parenthood without judgment or stigma. It means providing resources for parents to learn about emotional regulation, empathy, and healthy communication. By doing so, we can empower parents to break the cycle of emotional immaturity, offering them the opportunity to grow alongside their children.

Moreover, changing the narrative also involves acknowledging the resilience and strength of those who have grown up with emotionally immature parents. Many have had to navigate their emotional landscapes mainly independently, often becoming self-reliant and empathetic adults. Their stories are tales of struggle, profound personal development, and triumph. By honoring these journeys, we validate their experiences and provide hope and inspiration for others in similar situations.

In this reimagining of our societal story, we must also address the systemic barriers that prevent individuals from accessing the support they need. Economic disparities, social inequalities, and cultural differences can all impact a person's ability to seek help in developing emotional maturity. By advocating for inclusive, accessible mental health services and educational programs, we can begin to dismantle these barriers and create a more emotionally intelligent society.

As we endeavor to change the narrative, we must remember that this is not a task for the few but a mission for the many. It requires the collective efforts of educators, mental health professionals, policymakers, and communities to shift perceptions and create lasting change. Through this collaborative spirit, we can rewrite the story of parenting, one where emotional maturity is not just an aspiration but a reality for all.

Advocacy and Awareness

In the wake of recognizing the pervasive influence of emotionally immature parents on both individual lives and society at large, it becomes imperative to foster a culture of advocacy and awareness. The journey towards healing and societal change is not solitary; it requires collective acknowledgment and action.

Advocacy for the issues stemming from emotionally immature parenting begins with giving a voice to those affected. Many adults carry the invisible scars of their childhood experiences, often without realizing the source of their struggles. By creating platforms where these stories can be shared, we validate individual experiences and illuminate the common patterns that emerge in the lives of emotionally immature parents. This collective storytelling can break the silence surrounding this topic, encouraging others to come forward and seek the support they need.

Awareness, on the other hand, is a broader societal endeavor. It involves educating the public about the characteristics and consequences of emotional immaturity in parents. Awareness campaigns can take many forms, from public service announcements to social media campaigns, each designed to inform and enlighten the general populace. The goal is to shift the cultural perception, making it widely known that emotional immaturity is not a personal failing of the child but a behavioral pattern of the parent that can be addressed and improved upon.

Moreover, advocacy and awareness go hand in hand with professional development. Mental health professionals, educators, and social workers need to be equipped with the tools to recognize the signs of emotional immaturity in parents and support the children and adults affected by it. Training programs and continuing education courses can be instrumental in spreading this knowledge, ensuring that those in helping professions are prepared to intervene effectively and compassionately.

In the realm of policy, advocacy can lead to the development of support systems and legal frameworks that protect and assist children and families dealing with the impacts of emotionally immature parenting. This could include the implementation of parenting programs that emphasize emotional intelligence and resilience, as well as the provision of resources for children and adults seeking to heal from their childhood experiences.

The path forward is one of proactive engagement and empathy. By advocating for understanding and awareness, we can begin to dismantle the stigma associated with the repercussions of being raised by emotionally immature parents. Through these concerted efforts, we hope to see a future where emotional maturity is not just a personal virtue but a societal norm, where families can thrive in an environment of emotional health and well-being.

Educational Initiatives

Now, we must recognize the pivotal role of education. Educational initiatives provide the bedrock for equipping individuals with the knowledge and skills necessary to foster emotional maturity in personal and communal contexts.

The essence of such initiatives is not merely the transmission of information but the cultivation of environments where emotional intelligence is valued and nurtured. To this end, schools and educational institutions can play a transformative role. By integrating emotional literacy into curricula, educators can provide students with the tools to understand and manage their emotions and recognize and respond to the emotional needs of others.

One of the foundational steps in this educational endeavor is incorporating social and emotional learning (SEL) programs. These programs are designed to teach children from a young age about self-awareness, self-management, social awareness, relationship skills, and responsible decision-making. By embedding these competencies into the education fabric, children can develop a more nuanced understanding of their emotional landscape and that of others.

Furthermore, parent education programs are essential in breaking the cycle of emotional immaturity. These programs allow parents and caregivers to learn about healthy emotional development, effective communication strategies, and ways to build strong, empathetic relationships with their children. Providing support and resources can empower parents to model emotional maturity, setting a positive example for the next generation.

In addition to formal education settings, community-based workshops and online resources can extend the reach of these teachings. Public seminars and digital platforms can offer adults access to further their understanding of emotional maturity. Through these channels, the principles of emotional intelligence can permeate various aspects of society, from the workplace to family life.

Moreover, professional development for educators and mental health professionals is crucial. Training programs that emphasize the importance of emotional maturity can enhance the ability of these professionals to support not only the children in their care but also the parents who may struggle with their emotional growth.

In fostering educational initiatives that prioritize emotional maturity, we are investing in the well-being of our communities. By equipping individuals with the understanding and skills to navigate the complexities of emotional interactions, we lay the groundwork for healthier relationships and a more compassionate society. As we move forward, it is our collective responsibility to ensure that these educational efforts are inclusive, comprehensive, and reflective of the diverse needs of our communities.

Building Emotionally Mature Communities

In the quest to nurture emotionally mature communities, we must look beyond the confines of formal education and consider the broader tapestry of societal influences that shape our emotional development. The family unit, often the first social structure we encounter, plays a pivotal role. When parents are emotionally immature, they may inadvertently instill similar patterns in their children, perpetuating a cycle that can ripple through communities.

To break this cycle, we must foster environments that encourage emotional growth, not just in children but in adults as well. This calls for a cultural shift that values emotional intelligence alongside academic and professional achievements. We can begin by creating community programs offering support and resources for parents who want to develop their emotional maturity. These include workshops on effective communication, empathy, emotional regulation, and support groups where parents can share experiences and strategies.

Moreover, we must recognize that emotional maturity is not a destination but a journey. Communities can benefit from promoting lifelong learning in the emotional realm. Just as we might attend a gym to maintain physical health, we could benefit from regular 'emotional fitness' sessions to enhance our emotional well-being. These could be public lectures, meditation groups, or art and music therapy sessions designed to cultivate self-awareness, compassion, and resilience.

In addition, local governments and organizations can play a crucial role by integrating emotional maturity into their policies and practices. This might involve training community leaders and public servants in emotional intelligence, ensuring they can lead by example and make decisions considering the emotional well-being of the populations they serve.

It is also essential to provide accessible mental health services within communities. By removing the stigma around seeking help and making it easy and affordable to access therapists and counselors, we can encourage individuals to work on their emotional issues before they impact their parenting or other areas of community life.

Finally, the media and entertainment industries have a powerful influence on societal norms and values. By promoting narratives that showcase emotionally mature behavior, these industries can help shift public perception and inspire individuals to aspire to more incredible emotional growth.

Building emotionally mature communities requires a collective effort and a willingness to invest in the emotional health of all members. It is a process that will take time to happen. Still, with dedication and compassion, we can create a society where emotional intelligence is cherished and nurtured, allowing future generations to thrive in a more understanding, empathetic, and emotionally aware world.

Chapter Summary

- Emotional immaturity in parents affects society, including education, workplaces, and cultural narratives about parenting.
- In schools, children of emotionally immature parents may struggle with anxiety, peer relationships, and authority, impacting the learning environment.
- Adults from such backgrounds may face professional relationships and self-esteem difficulties, affecting workplace cohesion and productivity.
- Emotionally immature parenting perpetuates cycles of emotional dysfunction, hindering societal emotional intelligence and resilience.
- Media portrayals of parenting often lack nuance, creating unrealistic expectations and stigmatizing struggles, making it harder to seek help.
- The economic cost of emotional immaturity is significant, with increased reliance on mental health services and social support programs.
- Changing societal narratives around emotional maturity involves acknowledging parents' emotional growth journeys and providing support.
- Advocacy and awareness are crucial for addressing the impact of emotionally immature parenting, requiring collective action and policy changes.

EMBRACING EMOTIONAL MATURITY

Personal Reflections

As we draw near to the close of this exploration into the world shaped by emotionally immature parents, I find myself pausing to reflect on the personal journeys that have intersected with the pages of this book.

Each story shared and each insight gained has illuminated the challenges faced and cast a hopeful light on the path to emotional maturity.

In the quiet moments of introspection, I am reminded that understanding emotional immaturity is not just an academic pursuit. It is deeply personal. For many, it resonates with the echoes of childhood experiences, the struggles of navigating relationships, and the arduous journey toward self-awareness and healing. The courage displayed by those who have shared their stories with me, and by extension with you, the reader, is nothing short of inspirational. Their vulnerability has opened the door to a collective healing process that extends beyond the individual to touch the lives of others.

It is in these personal reflections that we find the seeds of change. Recognizing the traits of emotional immaturity in our parents is not an end but a beginning. It is the first step in a transformative process that allows us to break free from the cycles of the past. By acknowledging the pain, the confusion, and the longing for what might have been, we permit ourselves to seek a different narrative for our lives.

The journey towards emotional maturity is not a solitary one. It is a path we walk together, learning from each other's experiences and supporting our growth. As we embrace the complexities of our emotions, we learn to navigate them with grace and understanding. We learn that to be emotionally mature is not to be devoid of emotion but to engage with our feelings healthily and constructively.

This personal growth has a profound impact on how we raise our children, how we interact with our peers, and how we contribute to society. By striving for emotional maturity, we set a new standard for ourselves and those who seek guidance. We become beacons of stability and empathy, capable of nurturing relationships built on mutual respect and genuine connection.

As we move forward, let us carry the lessons learned and shared wisdom. Let us be gentle with ourselves as we navigate the complexities of our emotional landscapes. And remember that every step taken towards emotional maturity is a step towards a more compassionate and understanding world.

In the next section, we will explore how these personal transformations can ripple outward, creating waves of change that reach far beyond our immediate circles. The journey continues, and we contribute to a legacy of emotional health and resilience for generations with each step.

The Ripple Effect of Change

It is essential to recognize the profound influence our transformation can have on the world around us. This change, although deeply personal, does not occur in isolation. It sends out ripples that touch the lives of others, often in ways we cannot foresee.

The path to emotional maturity is marked by increased self-awareness, empathy, and the ability to foster healthy relationships. As individuals break the cycle of emotional immaturity, they become role models for others. Friends, siblings, and acquaintances may witness this evolution and find inspiration to embark on their journeys of self-discovery and healing.

Moreover, the shift towards emotional maturity within a family can have a transformative effect on its dynamics. Children who grow up with parents committed to their emotional development benefit from a stable and nurturing environment. This foundation equips them with the emotional intelligence and resilience necessary to navigate life's challenges more effectively.

In the broader context of society, embracing emotional maturity contributes to creating communities that value emotional intelligence and mental well-being. Workplaces can become more compassionate and supportive; schools can implement programs that prioritize the emotional development of students, and social policies can be crafted with a deeper understanding of the human psyche.

The ripple effect of change also extends to the cultural narrative around parenting and emotional health. As more individuals speak openly about their experiences and the importance of emotional maturity, there is a gradual shift in societal expectations and norms. This openness paves the way for future generations to approach parenting and personal development with greater awareness and intentionality.

Ultimately, the journey toward emotional maturity is not just about healing from the past; it's about creating a legacy of emotional health that will benefit future generations. It is a testament to the human spirit's capacity for growth and the enduring impact that one person's transformation can have on the fabric of society.

Hope for Future Generations

As we draw the curtains on our exploration of emotionally immature parents, we find ourselves standing at the threshold of a new era. In this era, the seeds of emotional maturity can be sown for the benefit of future generations. The journey through understanding the complexities of emotional immaturity in parents has been arduous yet enlightening, and it is with a heart full of hope that we look forward to the possibilities that lie ahead.

Hope, as a beacon, shines brightest in the aftermath of struggle. The awareness and insights gained from the preceding chapters will empower individuals to break the cycles of emotional immaturity that have, for too long, been passed down through generations. This hope is not a passive wish but a call to action—to embrace the responsibility of nurturing emotional growth within ourselves and our communities.

The prospect of raising emotionally mature generations begins with the individual. It starts with the conscious decision to embark on a journey of self-reflection and healing. For those who have experienced the challenges of having emotionally immature parents, this may mean seeking support, engaging in therapy, or finding solace in communities that understand their plight. It is through these personal transformations that the foundation for change is built.

Moreover, the hope for future generations is fortified by knowing that emotional maturity can be learned and cultivated. Parents, educators, and caregivers who understand emotional development can actively foster environments where children are encouraged to express their feelings, develop empathy, and build resilience. By modeling emotional maturity—expressing emotions healthily, setting boundaries, and practicing self-care—adults can provide invaluable lessons that children carry into adulthood.

The ripple effect of these individual changes is profound. As more people embrace emotional maturity, societal norms begin to shift. What was once a culture that may have inadvertently perpetuated emotional immaturity becomes one that values emotional intelligence and psychological well-being. This cultural shift can transform relationships, workplaces, and communities, leading to a more compassionate and empathetic world.

In this hopeful future, the legacy of emotional maturity is not just the absence of the negative traits associated with emotional immaturity but positive, nurturing relationships supporting the individual's holistic development. It is a future where emotional maturity is not an exception but a norm—a cherished value passed on with intention and care.

As we stand on the cusp of this hopeful horizon, we recognize that the journey does not end here. The conversation about emotional maturity is ongoing, and it is through continued dialogue and education that progress is made. Each step taken towards emotional maturity, no matter how small, is a step towards a brighter, more emotionally intelligent future for all generations.

Continuing the Conversation

As we draw near the conclusion of this journey, it is essential to recognize that the dialogue surrounding emotionally immature parents does not end with the turning of the last page. Much like the process of personal growth and healing, the conversation is ongoing. It is a continuous exchange of experiences, insights, and support that extends beyond the confines of this book and into the living fabric of our daily lives.

Embracing emotional maturity is not a destination but a path we walk daily. It is a commitment to self-awareness, empathy, and the willingness to engage in the sometimes challenging process of personal development. For those who have grown up with emotionally immature parents, this path can be particularly arduous, as it often involves unlearning patterns and beliefs that have been deeply ingrained since childhood.

Yet, it is within this very challenge that opportunity lies. Each step taken towards understanding and healing is a step away from the shadows of the past and towards a future of emotional resilience. By continuing to converse about these experiences, we validate our feelings and struggles and pave the way for others to find their voice and begin their journeys toward healing.

The conversation can take many forms. It may be found in support groups and therapy sessions, in the quiet confidences shared between friends, or even in the stories we tell ourselves about who we are and aspire to be. In these exchanges, we find the strength to confront our vulnerabilities and the courage to challenge the legacies of emotional immaturity.

Remember, you are not alone in this. The shared narratives of those who have navigated similar waters are a beacon of hope and a testament to the human capacity for growth and change. By continuing the conversation, we foster a community that upholds emotional maturity as a valued ideal that is attainable and worth striving for.

As we move forward, let us carry with us the understanding that our past does not have to dictate our future. We have the power to redefine our relationships, set boundaries, and cultivate the emotional health we may have felt was missing in our formative years. In doing so, we heal ourselves and break the cycle, offering hope for future generations to live with greater emotional intelligence and connectedness.

The dialogue about emotionally immature parents is evolving, with each of us contributing to its depth and richness. Continuing the conversation ensures that this vital topic remains in the light, where it can be examined, understood, and transcended.

Final Words of Encouragement

As we draw the curtains on our exploration of emotionally immature parents and the journey toward emotional maturity, I hope that you have found solace, understanding, and a path forward within these pages. The road to healing and growth is seldom straight or free of obstacles, but it is a road that leads to a more prosperous, more fulfilling life.

If you have recognized the shadows of emotional immaturity in your upbringing, know that the awareness you now hold is a decisive first step. The light can guide you through the process of untangling the complex emotions and patterns woven into your life's fabric. It is okay to feel many emotions—anger, sadness, compassion, or relief. These feelings are valid and signposts on your emotional maturity journey.

Embracing emotional maturity is about understanding where we come from and where we choose to go. It is about making conscious choices that align with our values and sense of self. It is about setting boundaries with kindness and assertiveness and nurturing reciprocal and respectful relationships. Remember, emotional maturity is not a destination but a continual growth, learning, and self-reflection process.

As you move forward, carry the knowledge that you are not alone. Many have walked this path before you, and many will walk it after. There is strength in the shared human experience and power in the stories we tell. With all its complexity and nuance, your story is an integral part of this tapestry.

Take heart in that every step you take toward emotional maturity is a step toward a more authentic life. It is a courageous act to break the cycle of emotional immaturity that requires patience and self-compassion. Be gentle with yourself as you navigate this path, and remember to celebrate the small victories along the way.

In closing, I encourage you to hold onto hope. Hope for the relationships that can be healed, the personal growth that awaits, and the generational changes your emotional maturity can inspire. Your journey may inspire others to embark on their own, creating ripples of positive change that extend far beyond what you imagine.

Thank you for allowing me to be a part of your journey. May you move forward with a heart full of courage, a mind open to learning, and a spirit ready to embrace the beauty of emotional maturity.

Your Feedback Matters

As we reach the end of this book, I extend my heartfelt gratitude for your time and engagement. It's been an honor to share this journey with you, and I hope it has been as enriching for you as it has been for me.

If the ideas we've explored have sparked new thoughts, inspired change, or provided comfort, I'd really appreciate it if you could share your experience with others. Your feedback benefits me as an author and guides fellow readers in their quest for their next meaningful read.

To leave a review on Amazon, follow the QR code below. Your insights and reflections are invaluable; by sharing them, you contribute to a larger conversation that extends far beyond the pages of this book.

Thank you once again for your company on this literary adventure. May the insights you've gained stay with you, and may your continuous quest for knowledge be ever-fulfilling.

ABOUT THE AUTHOR

Essie Woodard is an author best known for her groundbreaking book series "Generational Healing." With a background in psychology and a passion for helping individuals break free from the chains of their past, Woodard has dedicated her career to exploring the complex realms of inherited family trauma and the challenges of dealing with emotionally immature parents. Her work offers insightful analysis, practical personal growth, and healing strategies, resonating with readers worldwide.